ABOUT THE AUTHOR

Terry Virgo is a respected Bible teacher, author, and widely traveled speaker. Pastor of Clarendon Church in Brighton, England, he also oversees a leadership team responsible for more than seventy nondenominational churches in Great Britain, as well as churches in India, South Africa, Switzerland, Holland, and Mexico. His books include *Men of Destiny*, *Enjoying God's Grace*, and *Restoration in the Church*, which has been translated into German, Dutch, and Chinese and will soon be available in French, Spanish, Portuguese, and Hungarian.

GOD KNOWS YOU'RE HUMAN

GOD KNOWS YOU'RE HUMAN

Terry Virgo

Cityhill Publishing
Columbia, Missouri

Cityhill Publishing
Columbia, Missouri
Published 1991.
Printed in the U.S.A.

98 97 96 95 94 93 92 91   5 4 3 2 1
ISBN   0-939159-22-8

ACKNOWLEDGEMENTS

Special thanks go to Mary Austin for her outstanding contribution to this book, first of all working through tape recordings of my preaching, and then typing and retyping the manuscript.

CONTENTS

ACKNOWLEDGEMENTS *vii*
INTRODUCTION 11

SECTION I

David: A Man After God's Heart

Chapter 1   THE ONE GOD CHOOSES   15
Chapter 2   WHO IS THIS PHILISTINE?   23
Chapter 3   A TIME OF PRUNING   29
Chapter 4   WAITING FOR GOD   37
Chapter 5   GOD'S MAN SPOILED   45
Chapter 6   A SINNER FORGIVEN   53
Chapter 7   A HOUSE FOR GOD   59
Chapter 8   BE STRONG AND COURAGEOUS   65

SECTION II

Elijah: A Man Like Us

Chapter 9   NOW ELIJAH. . .   75
Chapter 10   FAITH ON TRIAL   81
Chapter 11   INTO THE CRUCIBLE   87
Chapter 12   THE TROUBLER OF ISRAEL   91
Chapter 13   THE TROUBLE WITH TOLERATION   97
Chapter 14   ENCOUNTER ON CARMEL   103

Chapter 15   REACHING ROCK BOTTOM 109
Chapter 16   YOUR GENTLENESS MADE ME GREAT 115
Chapter 17   GO AND MAKE DISCIPLES 123
Chapter 18   THE BONDS OF RELATIONSHIP 131

SECTION III

Jonah: A Man Who Ran From God

Chapter 19   A PAROCHIAL PROPHET 139
Chapter 20   HOW CAN YOU SLEEP? 145
Chapter 21   A SECOND CHANCE 153
Chapter 22   A HAPPY ENDING? 161
Chapter 23   ALONE WITH GOD 169
Conclusion   LIMPING ARMY, INVINCIBLE
                COMMANDER 177

THREE ORDINARY PEOPLE

Often we can learn more about God through reading stories than by studying concepts. We sometimes struggle with a principle, but we can quickly identify with a person. God has revealed himself not only through his words, but also by his actions. The Bible is not only a book about God; it's essentially about him in relation to human beings.

David, Elijah, and Jonah were three ordinary people. Each of them had plenty of reason to throw in the towel. They knew what it was like to stand alone, as well as to experience the dizzying heights of success. If you are conscious of your own limitations and fallibility, you have a choice. You can give up, resigning yourself to a lifetime of ineffectiveness. You can strive and push yourself until you collapse, exhausted. Or you can learn from people like David, Elijah, and Jonah, who discovered that God uses the weak to display his strength and reveal his glory.

It's my prayer that, as you read these pages, the characters will step off the page and become three-dimensional and relevant to your life today. Their weaknesses and temptations are not concealed, but neither is the grace of God that helped them prevail, sometimes against overwhelming odds.

The point of these stories is that God took hold of three vulnerable people and accomplished amazing things through them. God wants you to know that if he can use people like this, he can certainly use you as clear proof that his strength is made perfect in weakness.

God is never shocked by your humanity. He knows you're human, and he knows just how to encourage you and use you for his glory. You don't have to become an angel before God can use you. Enjoy your humanity and enjoy the constant availability of God's grace.

DAVID:
A MAN AFTER
GOD'S HEART

"I have found David the son of Jesse, a man after my heart, who will do all my will."

— Acts 13:22, NASB

CHAPTER 1

THE ONE GOD CHOOSES

David and Goliath's story must be one of the most exciting in the whole Bible. Many people who know almost nothing about Christianity can still tell you about the encounter between the young Israelite and the fearsome Philistine.

All the ingredients of high drama are there. A young man emerges from nowhere, strides into the midst of an army which is apparently paralyzed with fear, and with a seemingly foolish boldness declares his contempt for the enemy. Then, all alone and armed with the most primitive of weapons, he defeats the battle-hardened champion of the opposing forces, hands victory on a plate to his own side, and transforms their abject defeat into glorious triumph.

A heartening story—but what does it teach us? Let's look at the historical backdrop so we can fully appreciate the drama.

David grew up at a time when Israel was languishing spiritually. At one time Saul had been empowered by the Spirit and had led Israel into a resounding victory over the Ammonites. Now, however, through disobedience and unbelief, he had forfeited his right to lead God's chosen nation. Although he retained his position as king, God no longer recognized him as such.

The army, as well, was bereft of God's mighty presence. Shouting war cries and parading in full battle array was easy, but defeating Goliath presented a real problem. The soldiers squirmed in humiliation whenever he came into view.

This Philistine must have been a terrifying sight. Imagine ten feet of muscle and arrogant might, armed to the teeth with a spear the size of a weaver's beam and a sword that would be famous for years to come. No wonder the onlookers turned to jelly. No wonder no one responded when he roared out his challenge: "Choose a man for yourselves and let us fight together!" Whoever won in this single combat would gain the victory for the entire army: a great idea from the Philistines' point of view, but Israel's captains were not too thrilled with it, to say the least.

After the challenge had been issued, was there suddenly a long line at sick bay each morning? Were the usually robust soldiers unaccountably afflicted with bad backs and stomach aches? As Goliath roared and taunted every day for forty days, there were probably many debates about what to do and whom to send; but none of Saul's captains stood forth.

The number forty is often associated with times of trial in the Bible. The Israelites were tested for forty years in the wilderness. Jesus overcame Satan's temptations after forty days in the desert. And here, after Goliath had repeated his challenge for forty days, the army still had no answer.

God had already chosen a man

Daily Goliath ridiculed his enemies as he cried, "Choose a man for yourselves." Unknown to the Israelites, though, God had already chosen the man. Seeing the low state of his people, he had been preparing a remedy.

God had previously said to the prophet Samuel, "Go to Bethlehem, for I have chosen a man." When we are choosing men for ourselves, we must make sure that they are men whom God has already chosen for himself. God is in the business of choosing men for himself, and he wants us to see how he does it. What, then, led up to his choice of David?

Samuel, the prophet, was grief-stricken over Saul's failure to be the God-honoring king required to rule Israel. Now, though, a new word came to him: "Stop grieving for Saul. Fill your horn with oil, for I am sending you to Jesse of Bethlehem: I have chosen one of his sons to be king." Samuel obediently journeyed to one of the strangest nomination proceedings ever.

As Jesse's sons stood before him, Samuel could not fail to be impressed by the eldest son, Eliab. "Surely," he thought, "the Lord's anointed is before me." But, much to Samuel's surprise, God rejected him.

Samuel had previously anointed Saul, who had been a fine, strong, handsome young man, literally standing head and shoulders above everyone else. If this was God's previous choice, Samuel now expected to anoint a man of similar stature. He had not learned that God's choice has nothing to do with a person's stature. "Man looks on the outward appearance, but God looks on the heart."

Jesse called his second son, Abinadab, but God vetoed him too—as well as the third, Shammah, and the other four in turn. Perplexed, Samuel asked, "Are these all your children?" Jesse replied, "Actually, I do have one more son, but he's only a youngster and he's looking after the sheep." On Samuel's command, Jesse sent for David. Eventually, the young man who would change the history of Israel came before the old prophet with a freshness and inner beauty that could not be hidden. The Lord said to Samuel, "Arise, anoint him. He is the one." As Goliath was publicly shouting "Choose a man," God was secretly making his choice.

But how does God choose people? The passage of Scripture that tells us the most about what God is looking for is 1 Corinthians 1:26-29. Let's examine these verses word by word.

The foolish

First we are told, "God chose the foolish things of the world.

Not many wise are chosen." So many Christians write themselves off because they are not intellectuals. "I'm not as bright as everone else," they say. "I have virtually no academic qualifications, and you need that to succeed in the world. I really have nothing to offer." With this attitude, they often throw in the towel. But the Bible has excellent news for such people. It says quite plainly that God deliberately chose the foolish to shame the wise. He has planned to save the world through a foolish gospel—a gospel which provokes the wisdom of the intelligent.

When confronted with the gospel, the modern intellectual often replies, "You don't really expect me to believe that events in Palestine some two thousand years ago have anything to do with the world now, do you? What possible connection could there be between an obscure teacher from Nazareth and the major problems on our doorstep? You should be talking about pressing political issues such as world famine, oppression and warfare in Latin America, and the injustices of South Africa. But you narrow-minded Christians prefer to spread silly stories about Adam and Eve, heaven and hell, a cross, and a man who rose from the dead. It's all nonsense."

Intellectuals often struggle with the gospel, but God has chosen foolish people. If you consider yourself lacking in brain power, don't write yourself off. Instead, rejoice! Maybe you didn't excel at school. Maybe you feel like an academic failure. But do you believe what God says in his Word? A lot of scholarly people have terrible difficulty accepting the Bible. They can analyze it and give you a lot of theories about how it came to be written, about supposed sources and origins. But while they are minutely examining the manuscripts, you can be in touch with the Author. So don't write yourself off; instead, listen to Jesus. He said, "I praise you, Father, Lord of heaven and earth, because you have hidden these things from the wise and learned, and revealed them to little children. Yes, Father, for this was your good pleasure" (Matt. 11:25,26).

If you have a humble heart, God will make himself known to you. If you are "foolish," you can say, "I've got a head start." But if you are very intelligent, watch out. Not many wise are chosen, for worldly wisdom is a stumbling block. God will reveal himself from the least to the greatest. Note that the least are ahead. To enter the Kingdom of God everyone has to become like a little child. So before God can use strong people he has to weaken and humble them.

The weak

I expect you have heard people say, "Wouldn't it be wonderful if so-and-so were saved. He's so dynamic. He could do so much for the Lord." But consider this: "God chose the weak things of the world to shame the strong." He did not choose many mighty and influential people. We think in a totally different way from God. Impressed as we are by human personality and magnetism, our ideal Christians are prominent sportsmen, famous pop stars, and attractive media people, because of what they are in themselves. Sadly, though, God cannot choose many mighty individuals for fear that they will glory in their own abilities. Their personalities and accomplishments can get in the way, preventing people from seeing God's power and glory. The truth is that God has to deal with the mighty so that they become aware of their weakness; then he can fill them with his power and use them.

Jacob, for example, was a clever rascal who knew how to wheel and deal, and he used his cunning to his own advantage. God said, "I love him anyway and I'm going to use him." But first Jacob had to be weakened. His "hip operation" left him limping for the rest of his life—a constant reminder of his human frailty and fallibility.

God had plans for Moses, too. As a baby he was rescued from the river Nile and brought up by Pharaoh's daughter. Educated and trained at Egypt University, he became "mighty in word and deed," a prince—handsome, privileged, wealthy, resourceful, and intelligent. In short, a superb candidate for leadership. So what did God do? He sent Moses into the desert, fleeing for his life, and there broke his self-importance and self-reliance. When

God eventually did call him and revealed his plan for his life, all Moses could say was, "You must have the wrong person. How could someone like me talk to Pharaoh?"

Peter confidently boasted, "The rest may fail you, but I never will!" Not long afterwards he swore that he had never known Jesus, and subsequently was overwhelmed with regret. He went through a painful, deeply humbling experience, only to be totally reinstated through the mercy and grace of his Lord. So if you are weak, don't feel disqualified, but instead rejoice; and if you are strong, be prepared to go through some buffeting—or else humble yourself, because God chooses and uses the weak.

The base

As we proceed through the list, we next find that "not many are of noble birth." Instead, God prefers the lowly and the outsiders. Some people place a lot of importance on family background and associations. They like to be "in" with the "right" people or to have friends higher up on the social ladder.

But not many noble people are chosen. Pride of place is a major obstacle to entering the kingdom, so if you are from "good stock," you may be lucky to get in at all! God chooses the base— people whom nobody else wants to befriend. The Jews would spit at a tax collector as they walked past him, but Jesus called such a man and went for a meal in his home.

Some of us are ashamed of our backgrounds. When I was at secondary school, our funny little caretaker was the object of much ridicule from the boys. When you're a teenager you can be rather arrogant and snobbish, and the custodian was regarded as having about as much importance as the rubbish bins he lifted around. So it was not surprising that, at that time, I was not too quick to divulge what my father did for a living. People knew I lived in the grounds of another school, and I didn't mind if they thought that my father was a teacher, or even a headmaster. Actually, he was a custodian, too. I was wary of letting others know that, though he was a wonderful father and I loved him dearly.

Perhaps you don't want people to know about your background. Maybe you are ashamed of your roots. Take heart: God has personally selected people of "no family." You who were no people are now God's people!

The despised

"God chose... the despised things." One commentary defines the word "despised" as "expressly branded with contempt." The same word is used in Luke 23:11: "The soldiers treated him with contempt and mocked him." They looked on this Jesus, this religious fanatic, as a stupid fool, and they despised him.

Some of us are despised in our own eyes, let alone in the eyes of anyone else. We despise ourselves because we have gotten used to thinking of ourselves as nothings. It's as if people were saying, "We don't have time for you. We're getting on with more important things."

The "are nots"

Finally, we reach the end of this downward spiral: "He chose... the things that are not." These are the people who are overlooked, those who don't count or even figure in anyone's thinking. Are you like this in your church? Does no one ever speak to you after the Sunday meeting? Everyone else seems to be talking and laughing together. They are happy in a crowd, but you aren't. You feel uneasy, awkward. You are used to slipping away quietly. You think, "Nobody really wants to talk to me, and it gets embarrassing just standing there. They seem to be able to cope, but I can't." The devil says all sorts of horrible things to you about how insignificant you are. "You're nothing. Why do you bother to come? No one notices whether you're there or not. When you're sick, nobody comes to visit."

The story of David tells us, though, that God has chosen the people who are overlooked, those who seem to have no significance at all. Picture Samuel, the great national leader, inviting Jesse and his sons to a sacrifice. What a privilege! If I thought that Queen Elizabeth was going to come to my home, I would want all of my family there. But Jesse disregarded David as though his youngest son did not exist.

Have you been overlooked by your father? Does he ignore you? Perhaps he has since died, but when he was alive, you never registered with him. He was always indifferent to you. Maybe you carried the rejection for a long time. Do you feel that no one has ever really loved you, that nobody really cares at all?

Perhaps to Jesse seven was the perfect number. David was number eight, and he was left out. Maybe some of you are like that: Mom and Dad thought they had finished, and then you turned up. Some of you feel you are a nuisance and you have been told so. Some of you were even told by your parents, "We didn't want you. I wish you had never come."

"Here are my seven sons," said Jesse. Samuel might never have known about David; but David was God's choice. God chose an apparently irrelevant person to turn a nation upside down.

Are you irrelevant? Maybe you tell yourself, "It doesn't much matter if I'm included." Do you even avoid attending gatherings because you don't know how you will cope? You feel you are of no consequence and have nothing to offer. You despise yourself. You are not worthy of any attention, and you can't keep up with everyone else.

But God has chosen the "are nots" to throw down the things that are. You can't get any lower than an "are not" —a thing that doesn't exist. God chose David to bring to naught a certain Goliath, of whose significance there was no doubt. If you are a believer, God has chosen you and even now wants to destroy the giants of fear and rejection that have cast their shadow over your life. Why don't you refuse the devil's lies and taunts and take hold of God's Word? Say to yourself, and to anybody else who wants to listen, "I am God's choice. He chose me before he made the world. By his power I am strong, and by his grace I count in his plan! God cares for me, and he is going to use me.

CHAPTER 2

WHO IS THIS PHILISTINE?

Goliath looked down on the Israelites with contempt. "We Philistines," he mused, "have already conquered the Moabites, and this little nation is just the next obstacle in our path." He was totally unaware that there was another factor to be taken into account: he was confronting not just another little nation but God's covenant people.

The perspective

David understood. He bore the covenant mark of circumcision in his body. He had an advantage over everyone else, regardless of their prowess or prestige. He was one of the people of God!

Doubtless, as Goliath prepared to go out each morning, he looked at his ten-foot reflection in his mirror, adjusted his ton of armor, and admired his impressive physique. "What a marvelous specimen I am! Now let's go out and shake up those Israelites again."

But David didn't see Goliath as the giant saw himself. As this hulking figure strutted out to display his might and roar out his challenge, David remained totally unimpressed. Turning to his brothers, he asked, "Who is this uncircumcised Philistine?" Whatever Goliath's strengths were, he was a heathen: God was not with him.

David had a big view of God, by which he measured everything else. He had seen enough of God's handiwork to cut everything else down to size. "This is God's battle; we're God's army. We have God's covenant promises. Goliath may be an awesome foe, but he must fall before the living God."

Like the Israelites, many of us see our Goliaths before we see God. We cower before the enemy, certain of defeat, and think that we must somehow try to bring God into the situation to help us scrape together at least a few small blessings before catastrophe strikes.

I once heard a story about a man named Bhakt Singh. Someone had told him of an unforgettable sight—Mount Everest at the break of dawn. So, in a state of high expectation, he joined some others who were also eager to see this phenomenon. They set out early one morning while it was still dark and arrived at the viewing point, where they waited for the sunrise.

Dawn broke. There was the mountain. Everyone gazed at it and made appropriate noises of wonder and awe. Everyone, that is, except Bhakt Singh. As the others began to leave, he turned to the guide and shared his disappointment. "Wait here for about twenty minutes," replied the guide. So while the rest of the party made their way back down, he stayed on.

After a short time, the early morning mist in the valley began to clear. Suddenly the view became more distinct. Then it seemed as though the whole mountain took a gigantic step forward, revealing itself in all its towering majesty and splendor. The sight was overwhelming. Bhakt Singh later said, "There are twenty people somewhere in the world who believe they saw Mount Everest at dawn. I have to testify that they really didn't see it at all."

There are a lot of people today who say, "We know the Lord," but whenever some problem, some Goliath, looms up, it is too much for them to handle. Why was David not intimidated by Goliath? Because he had seen something: Goliath was mighty, but God was mightier. David had such a view of this covenant-keeping God that he had no difficulty in believing that an uncircumcised Philistine must fall before him.

Paul prayed for the churches "...that the glorious Father may give you the Spirit of wisdom and revelation, so that you may know him better... that the eyes of your heart may be enlightened in order that you may know the hope to which he has called you, the riches of his glorious inheritance in the saints, and his incomparably great power for us who believe" (Eph. 1:17-19).

We must not simply learn the jargon, praising the view when all we've seen is a cloud-obscured mountain, leaving us to wonder what else there is to experience. No. Like Paul, we must get on our knees and pray, "Lord, open our eyes to see what you're really like." Then God can reveal to us his glory; then we will be changed people; and then all our Goliaths will have to step aside.

David, though apparently ignored by his father and his brothers, had a secret history with God. He had an insatiable appetite for fellowship with him. While Samuel had looked on Eliab's appearance, God had seen David's heart and had enjoyed fellowship with him.

David was hungry for God's approval alone. Maybe in his loneliness on the hillsides with the sheep he looked up at the sky and the stars and began seeking God. "I want to know you, God. You're my exceeding joy. You're my light and my salvation. In your presence there's fullness of joy, and at your right hand there are pleasures forever more. I want to know you."

This young man had a passion for God, and God loves people like that. They might be weak and despised—"nobodies" in the world's eyes—but they want God. These are the people whom God actually delights to commend. Jesus said, "How can you believe if you accept praise from one another, yet make no effort to obtain the praise that comes from the only God?" (John 5:44).

God commended David. Does he commend you? Do you want God's approval? It is so easy to say that you do, but then find yourself manipulating things to gain recognition and praise from men: "If only I could get into that setting. If only I could be acknowledged by that person. If only I could get to that situation, that job, that party, that meeting, that platform, it would be to my advantage. I would be known, recognized." God delights in people who are indifferent to such strategies, who say instead, "Father, have I walked with you today? Have I pleased you?"

God said about David, "I have found a man after my own heart." If you want God's praise, tell him, "I want your approval more than anything else in the world," and mean it. Then he can respond, "That's my son, with whom I am well pleased." Then, when one day you stand before him, God's "Well done, son" will not be foreign to you. You will have sensed it many times before.

The battle

When, after forty days, David slew Goliath, the defeated army of Israel suddenly became totally victorious. Without lifting a finger, they became the beneficiaries of David's courageous one-man exploit. By his victory their situation was totally changed. Now they were on the winning side.

This contest reminds us of another battle in which losers became winners through the triumph of one man. Jesus, who stood in our behalf to destroy the works of the devil, fought a lonely battle to conquer our enemy. Initially, Jesus' death completely devastated his disciples, who scattered and did not know what to do with themselves. Then suddenly they realized that their Master was alive. Jesus' resurrection turned a band of despondent failures into an army of victorious soldiers who turned the world upside down.

How do defeated individuals triumph? They come into the fruits of Jesus' victory. Jesus conquered the devil. He has destroyed principalities and powers, triumphing gloriously over them in the cross. God wants us to stand David-like with full assurance of faith as we face our enemies.

David did not defeat Goliath by relying on his own strength. He fought the battle by his faith in God. He knew that it was God's battle and went in God's name. "I come against you in the name of the Lord," he said. And he overcame the enemy with a single stone!

David's stones were like guaranteed promises from God. We can imagine him going down to the brook to gather them, saying to himself, "I will kill Goliath, but I just need five covenant promises from God." Stones tend to look very ordinary out of water, but under water they display patterns of great beauty. As David picked out the stones, it was as though he picked up promises from God's Word over which the water of the Holy Spirit had run, making them real, sharp, and powerful for hurling against his foe.

What Spirit-anointed promises would God give us if we were standing in front of Goliath, listening to him curse us by his gods? How about some of these: "There is no divination that will prosper against Israel"; "I will never fail you nor forsake you"; "Greater is he who is in you than he who is in the world"; "I will always lead you in triumph." All these would suffice, but I can imagine David saying, "I have found just the stone I need: 'No man shall be able to stand before you.'"

Goliath might have been a giant, but he was only a man. He would not be able to stand before one empowered by God. That was the promise. David had to be a winner. This giant would not be allowed to defy the armies of the living God.

Our greatest need is to see God, to recognize that everything that stands against us is nothing compared to his covenant promises. "Who is this uncircumcised Philistine?" He is not one of God's covenant people; therefore he cannot stand.

Goliath did not stand. David knocked him down and then finished the job by cutting off his head.

If we do not take our battles through to total victory, we will leave a gap that the enemy will exploit. There are three places where Joshua did not completely prevail in battle: Gaza, Ashdod, and Gath (Josh. 11:22). Interestingly enough, there was later rebellion in each of these places. Samson died in Gaza (Judg. 16:21-30); the men of Ashdod received the stolen ark from the Israelites in another tragic defeat (1 Sam. 5:1); and guess who was born in Gath—Goliath! (1 Sam. 17:4).

Our Goliaths must not merely be knocked unconscious, they must be well and truly put to death! We must have no mercy upon them. We must not only love righteousness, but also hate evil and destroy it wherever it confronts us. Every taunt from the enemy must be overcome. You must take God's promises of victory and hurl them with faith at your enemy every time he tries to tell you that he has you cornered. Ask God to make his promises mighty in your heart. Fear is the substance of things dreaded, but "faith is the substance of things hoped for" (Heb. 11:1, NKJV).

The victory

The enemy tries to tell you that you are not strong enough to defeat him and that to get anywhere in life you must be wise, strong, noble, and influential—perhaps like Goliath appeared to his comrades. It's a lie. God has chosen people who are foolish, weak, base, and despised; and he has chosen you. He has loved you in your weakness because he delights to bring to naught things like Goliath.

Your giants will hurl cruel taunts at you: "You're stupid and feeble!" "You weren't wanted in the first place." "You're a nobody, and no one cares about you." You feel the wounds and despise yourself—but you needn't trail off dejected and despairing. God has given you his stones, his promises. He wants you to lift up your head, pick up those promises, and fling the truth at the enemy: "God has called me by name. He loves me. I'm chosen and precious, and I have a glorious inheritance! I'm going to move on with Jesus. I've lived with these negative feelings for years but I'm not going to put up with them any more. From now on I'm going to use the Word of God to overcome. I'm going to step out into the freedom and victory Jesus has won for me!"

CHAPTER 3

A TIME OF PRUNING

"The path of the righteous is like the first gleam of dawn, shining ever brighter till the full light of day."
— *Prov. 4:18*

When we first come to Christ, we emerge from darkness and are plunged into a wonderful new light. Whereas we once knew nothing about God, we suddenly find that now we can know him personally.

But the proverb given above says that this initial experience is just the first light. God's plan for each of us is that the dawn will be almost forgotten as we move on into the full glory of midday. God wants us to be transformed as we move from one degree of glory to another. What David came to discover, and what we will learn, is that the journey is not necessarily smooth. We do not always travel on a gentle, even path, ever upward in God. The landscape often more closely resembles a mountain range, and the trek can be difficult and demanding.

David seemed to burst onto the public scene with an immediate mountain-top experience. Coming from nowhere, he slew Goliath, went out with the armies of Saul, and very soon became a national hero, a real superstar. He won the hearts of the people of Israel and the singers sang of him, "David has slain his ten thousands." We wonder how things could have gotten brighter for him. In fact they would later become much brighter. God had great purposes for him, but his first lesson was that to get to the next peak, he had to go down into a valley.

Before David was to excel any further, God led him in an unexpected direction. He endured pressures that he could never have anticipated, yet which God used to develop his character and prepare him for the great task that lay ahead.

Opposition

David must have found it a great privilege to be promoted into Saul's army. No longer was he just a boy at home; he was now able to fight the king's battles, to serve the monarch whom he had always respected. He had an excellent attitude toward Saul. He never opposed, attacked, or brought dishonor to the king. He was, quite simply, a thoroughly devoted and obedient soldier.

Although David did not make trouble or seek it out, trouble still seemed to find him. It came, first of all, in the form of opposition. David might well have expected the opposition to come from Israel's enemies, from the armies that he was seeking to overthrow in the name of God. Instead, it arrived from a totally unexpected source: from Saul himself. Though the king should have been delighted with David's zeal and faithfulness, he was consumed by bitter envy and jealousy.

Saul is one of the saddest characters in the whole Bible. When Samuel found Saul he was not an arrogant man. He was humble, fair-minded, zealous, and courageous in battle. He was also anointed with the Spirit. He seemed an ideal choice for king, but he failed tragically. Knowing that he had been passed over, Saul grew increasingly hostile to David.

By contrast, when God anointed Samuel, the elderly Eli was wise enough to acknowledge that God was at work. Eli had failed God, but he managed to stand back and let Samuel's ministry emerge. Proud and bitter Saul, however, could never adopt such a stance. As David continued to be successful, Saul fumed.

Don't be offended when someone else is successful or when a younger Christian is promoted to a more prominent position than you. Instead, be ready to acknowledge the anointing of God and to respect the person whom God respects. Never speak against the individual whom God is pleased to choose.

Opposition always surfaces when someone has been raised up by God. Jesus experienced it and so have countless others through the ages. Seeing the power that attended the ministry of Whitefield and Wesley, the established church of their day publicly ridiculed these men for preaching in the open air. C.H. Spurgeon, the great Baptist preacher, was ridiculed, and William Booth of the Salvation Army was even labeled the Antichrist. The opposition against them might have been justified if they had been heretical. But these men were simply preaching the truth of God and experiencing his blessing.

It's strange, but it's a fact that one man's blessing so often leads to other men's hostility. David didn't look for trouble. He remained gracious, warm, and loving, but the antagonism still came and in the end he had to flee. So don't be surprised when others object to you. Don't look for opposition; just continue to live for God and trust him when you meet hostility. Also learn the lessons that come from the experience, because in the final analysis you are in God's hands, and he uses all circumstances for your good. "The Lord disciplines those he loves, and he punishes everyone he accepts as a son" (Heb. 12:6).

Pruning is protective

God, the great gardener, knows how to cut back his plantings in order to protect and guard them. David was never out of his sight. God was watching over his servant and stayed actively at work in his life. He knew that David was still a young man. If he continued to receive fame and adulation, would he be able to cope with it? Would he be able to withstand the many temptations and dangers that would come his way?

David went from national celebrity to living as a fugitive, holed up in a cave. In that setting he learned a great deal and ultimately emerged with a committed and disciplined army. God used the pruning to protect him from the spotlight.

A little while ago I saw on television an interview with a member of a famous rock group. He was over forty years old but he was still trying to work out what life was all about. At the time he was battling alcohol addiction. The problem began because he could not cope with the unexpected effects of international fame. He admitted, "I'm still living like a teenager."

Church history shows that apart from notable exceptions such as Whitefield, Spurgeon, and McCheyne, God has allowed few young men to be very prominent in his church. God loves his servants too much to give them that sort of responsibility too soon, so he protects them from it.

Pruning is painful

Pruning is inevitable. We are told in John 15 that God cuts the branch that bears fruit as well as the one that does not. All branches encounter the Lord and his knife. None of us can escape it: the fruitless he removes; the fruitful he prunes. Sometimes God seems to strip away some very precious things: people you love, a job that was important. Sometimes God almost breaks your heart when he prunes you.

I remember a time in my own life when I felt shut in, lonely, and sore because of God's pruning. I was in London, walking with a friend in Regent's Park. The rose bushes were all very short, no more than stubs in the ground. I remarked to my friend, "Look how they have ruined those rose bushes." He dispelled my ignorance. "To have good roses you must prune them right down," he said. I can still remember the strange sense of pain mixed with comprehension as he explained the process to me. Have you been through that, too? You feel cut back—a dry, leafless stub. Remember, though, that God knows what he is doing. Be patient and say with confidence, "Father, I receive it from your hands."

One minute David was riding into battle with brave, trained

soldiers on the right and left. The next minute he was in a little cave with the three "D's" —the Distressed, the in-Debt, and the Discontented—a motley crew, shut in, cut off.

You can be pruned in all sorts of ways. Perhaps you have moved to a new town. In your previous church you used to be an elder or a leader, but in this new church you have no such position of responsibility. Perhaps, as a single person, you were very independent, but now that you are married you are no longer so free to do what you want. You have to learn to build a relationship, and that means thinking about the other person's needs as well as your own. Perhaps you and your partner once enjoyed a great deal of freedom, but now you have children and all the time-consuming responsibilities they bring. Or, perhaps you or a member of your family were once healthy and active, but now illness has come and you are shut in.

David was shut in. Are you? Do you say, "O God, I envy the freedom and progress others have. Some of them are only young, but they're receiving such blessing from you. Why am I not? Why am I so cut back?" It's painful, isn't it? But God knows what he is doing with your life. It's time to trust him, because he has a reason for doing it.

A picture of obedience

Picture, for a moment, an imaginary scene that can help illustrate why God restrains us for our own benefit. Imagine a splendid carriage being pulled down the road by six fine-looking horses. The carriage stops, and the coachman alights to investigate an obstruction under one of the wheels. The horses, decorated with bells and plumes, look magnificent as they wait in the sun. At any moment they could bolt, crushing the man beneath the carriage. But the coachman shows no fear of that. He works calmly under the carriage, not a plume quivering or bell tinkling. Each horse stands obediently still.

Then two young colts come galloping up, over an open field. They are completely unrestrained and seem to challenge the carriage horses to join them in their liberty. But the temptation falls on deaf ears—the carriage horses make no sign of response. They just continue to stand calmly with the carriage and ignore the taunts of the colts.

Then, taking a rope in hand, the coachman catches the two colts, ties them to the carriage, and takes them to a corral where they begin to go through a period of training and discipline. Time passes and their forced confinement becomes increasingly tedious and frustrating. One colt, longing for the days when he roamed freely, feels that he can't take another day. He leaps the fence and gallops away to enjoy the grassy hills.

The other colt stays behind. Gradually he learns to yield and to respond to the whip and bridle. The training is tough, but he begins to understand why it's necessary. Finally, it ends. Is he then rewarded by being released to run free again? No. A harness is dropped around his shoulders, and he is more confined than ever! Now he can't even run around the corral; he can only move when his master speaks.

Sometime later, the first colt is nibbling grass on a hillside when down the road comes the king's carriage drawn by six horses. The colt looks up, amazed to see in the lead on the right his former stablemate, now grown strong and mature.

While the two colts were able to roam free they did not have the choice to rebel or submit. They were their own masters. But when they were tested and trained, it became clear which one was willing to submit and which was rebellious. It may seem safer to avoid discipline because of the risk of being found rebellious, but without discipline we cannot share in the glory of sonship.

When someone is first saved, he usually experiences a period of extraordinary freedom. The new convert seems to be able to get away with almost anything. You experience amazing answers to prayer, and even when you have done some questionable things, somehow God gets you off the hook. Then God says, "All right, time for the next phase." At this point you demonstrate by your reaction whether you have really learned to submit to God. Will you resist God-ordained restrictions or will you patiently submit and trust him?

We can picture that colt on the hillside running in circles and calling to his friend, "Come and join me! Come and enjoy the freedom!" Yes, this colt was free, but he was getting nowhere. The carriage horse was conscious of a deep sense of fulfillment and purpose. The one colt was weak, immature, and foolish compared with his strong, well trained colleague.

Christians will go through times of testing, in which they feel like they've been restrained in a corral. God will use those who are willing to undergo discipline, those who don't rebel when God says, "I am shutting you in. There is a purpose in it. Move when I tell you to move."

We're not free as Christians. We are slaves of the Lord Jesus Christ, and he wants us to respond positively to his training program. Do you receive the discipline of God? Are you willing to be shut in, or must you always be "free"? Do you make all your own decisions and do whatever you like, or have you found purpose in pruning, in being cut back? When God begins to bless you with fruit, do not be surprised when you suddenly feel his pruning knife. You are being cut back not because he no longer loves you, but because he wants you to bear even more fruit for him.

CHAPTER 4

WAITING FOR GOD

During stressful times other temptations can rear their ugly heads. Personal pain and frustration can cause unexpected character traits to surface.

The temptation to retaliate

It would have been easy for David to retaliate, to cry out in his cave against what he was experiencing, "This isn't fair! I haven't done anything wrong. Why should I be going through this?"

David handled himself magnificently. Even though he knew that Saul was the guilty party, David refused to speak against him or to retaliate in any way. Once, when Saul unwittingly came into the cave where David was hiding, David refused to take advantage of the situation and kill him. Instead, he cut off a piece of Saul's robe—and was later conscience-stricken even about that mildly insubordinate act. What a tender heart this fearless warrior had.

There in the cave, David came under considerable pressure to respond wrongly to the situation. He was the leader of a group of men who had not yet been disciplined in godliness and who were urging him, "Come on, David. Saul deserves to die. God has

37

given him into your hand. Now's your chance to finish him off!" Devotion to David drove them to say these things, but David would not listen.

How do you deal with the pressure to take matters into your own hands? There are sometimes dear friends who, out of loyalty, want to see justice done and urge you to take action to vindicate yourself. Sometimes, a wife can push her husband into taking steps that he shouldn't take.

King Ahab wanted to buy a vineyard from Naboth, who did not want to sell it. At this point, Ahab's wife intervened. She wanted to act for her husband, to make sure he was given the recognition due his position. "You're the king, aren't you? Well, it's about time people came to terms with that. Come on, pull some weight!"

A wife may not be wicked like Jezebel, but she can be anxious to see her husband esteemed. She knows how kind and generous he is, how hard he prays and how little recognition he gets. She wants to protect and encourage him, so she says, "It's not fair! You should have been honored."

Under this sort of pressure it is easy to react by uncovering the shortcomings of others, to speak poorly of them and expose their weaknesses. "Oh, he's a fine fellow, of course, but did you know about...?"

God is waiting to see how you respond to the temptation to retaliate. "Will you accept my discipline, my pruning? Will you prove yourself worthy of 'pulling my carriage' or do you only want to run free on the hillside and do whatever you like?" David faced a powerful temptation. Would he give in to the pressure from his followers and take revenge on Saul? No. He triumphed over temptation; and God could say, "I have found David a man after my own heart."

Did David ask himself, "Why does God allow Saul to remain on the throne? Why doesn't he have him killed in battle?" Whatever his thoughts, he realized that God was on the throne and refused to complain. Not only that, he also overcame the temptation to act in God's place, to "do God a favor" by getting Saul out of the way for good.

Maybe you don't understand what God is doing in your life. Maybe your heart is crying out, "Lord, it isn't fair! Why do I have to suffer while the guilty get off so lightly?" Resist the temptation to react. Fear God and leave things with him. Say to him, "Father, your ways are past finding out, but I'm going to trust and worship you in the midst of this." Then imagine God in heaven with your report card in his hand, saying, "You passed with flying colors."

The temptation to despair

David lamented, "One day I'll die at the hands of Saul." Clearly, the temptation to despair was very real for him. He was away from Israel, his homeland, and he thought, "I'll be killed. It's inevitable." He nearly gave up. But then he voiced that beautiful psalm: "I would have fainted if I had not believed to see the goodness of the Lord in the land of the living."

Many good people have nearly despaired and have cried out in desperation to God. Elijah prayed, "Take my life from me." Others, like Moses and Jeremiah, almost reached the place of suicide. Perhaps you have been overwhelmed by similar dark thoughts and have cried out, "Oh, God, I can't bear this!" But somehow God has given you the strength to go on.

Sometimes the pruning is hard. Maybe your fiance broke off your engagement or you've lost your job. Perhaps a loved one died suddenly. Maybe you had a disabling accident or discovered a close friend has cancer. In situations like these, we are tempted to despair. David nearly did. "Why have you rejected me?" he asked God. "Why must I go about mourning, oppressed by the enemy?" But he refused the temptation to give in to hopelessness. "Put your hope in God," he urged his soul, "for I will yet praise him, my Savior and my God."

The temptation to leave

It's tragic when a gifted young man begins a ministry, goes through difficulties, and then becomes tempted to throw the whole thing overboard.

The disciples discovered Jesus' words were not always easy to take. On one occasion, they grumbled to one another, "This is a hard teaching. Who can accept it?" Jesus, aware of the offense he had caused them and conscious that many of his disciples were walking away, turned to the twelve and asked, "Are you leaving as well?"

The temptation to leave must have been very strong. Jesus' teaching was offensive to many, and all around people were deserting him. "Are we really going to influence the world?" the disciples must have wondered. "When is this kingdom really going to break out? Sometimes I don't understand Jesus at all. It's so hard, and now he's giving us a chance to opt out."

Nevertheless, they turned down his offer. "Lord, to whom shall we go?" Peter replied. "You have the words of eternal life. We believe and know that you are the Holy One of God" (John 6:68,69).

Although puzzled and shaken, the disciples came right back to the foundations of their faith: this man is the Son of God. In the light of such a tremendous fact, where else is there to go?

David had been tempted to forsake Israel and join the Philistines. But he knew his roots were in the historical family of God. So although he had to live apart from God's people for a while, he never yielded to the temptation to finally dismiss them. Indeed, he expressed the most amazing love for Saul and the Israelites, even when they rejected him.

The dispirited "no-hopers" who first joined David steadily became more committed to him. As he loved them and trained them into a powerful fighting force, he must have thought of Saul and his ineffective army and been tempted to think, "We're the troops that God is going to use now. A plague on Saul and his men! I will form a new independent army. God isn't with them. He's with us."

David didn't leave his roots, though he longed to be back where he really belonged. God ultimately had not called him to lead a small exclusive army but to lead the whole nation. Similarly, today God does not want to move on just a small sect of believers, but to restore and revive the whole church on earth.

A Friend

David ultimately was rewarded for his obedience and endurance. In the meantime, he received some magnificent compensations. First, God gave him a friend, Jonathan, as well as a number of outstanding men.

As captain of Saul's army, David interacted mainly with soldiers. Later, in Adullum's cave, he gave himself to serve and lead the needy who gathered to him. Now he discovered a beautiful new relationship. God gave him a friend who loved him with deep devotion. David found in Jonathan a covenant brother, one who was totally committed to him.

We all have the need for intimate friendship. The church was never meant to be the gathering of strangers and mere co-workers. Paul spoke of his "beloved brothers" whom he "longed for." He used words that expressed deep affection, and tears often flowed when journeys kept these friends apart.

I have many covenant brothers. Our hearts are joined together. We love and respect one another, honor each other's God-given ministry, and feel secure in each other's loyalty. I really do not know how I would manage without them. Have you got brothers and sisters like that? Who can set a value on them?

Outstanding men

God also gave David a skillful volunteer army. Originally, it was 400 indebted, disillusioned men—just a handful of people in comparison with the thousands of trained soldiers David was accustomed to leading into battle. But he worked with what he had, training and fashioning them into a fighting unit. These "nobodies" loved David, and as they responded to his leadership, they began to reflect something of his character. As they developed into a crack unit, high-caliber men who were already trained were drawn to David's powerful anointing. God was doing something new in the land.

Amaziah was among those skilled warriors who defected to David. He was chief of the "thirty," and when the Spirit came upon him he declared, "We are yours, O David! We are with you,

O son of Jesse! Success, success to you, and success to those who help you, for your God will help you" (1 Chron. 12:18).

Some believers get very worried about that sort of statement. They fear the danger of such declarations of commitment. They are concerned that it could lead to a loss of personal freedom and that individuals will become weak, mindless sheep.

But the men who joined David were not spineless individuals; they were mighty and highly gifted men. "The least was a match for a hundred, and the greatest for a thousand" (1 Chron. 12:14). No one forced them to join David's army; he didn't "take over" these men; rather, they came to him. They recognized that God was with David, and although they were all gifted and strong in their own right, they were willing to lay aside their independence and put their great gifts at his disposal, declaring, "We are yours!"

David had the same attitude as Jesus: "All the Father has given me will come to me." A spiritual principle is in operation here. God anoints a leader, then others see God's hand on him and come to him, saying, "I want to join in what you are doing. I can see among those who follow you the benefits of your spiritual leadership, and I want to be in on it, too."

Some Christians would say, "You must disciple people to Jesus, not to yourself." That is right, of course, but the men who joined David didn't say, "We are yours, Jehovah!" They said, "We are yours, David." They were God's people, but by giving themselves to David they were also serving God's purpose.

We know that we are God's. We know that we must have a personal walk with him, but we are joined to others in the kingdom army and we establish God's purposes together. The Bible says it was the Holy Spirit who came on Amaziah and inspired him to say "we are yours" to David. It is the same Holy Spirit who gives us all the faith to take similar action.

Have you committed yourself to anyone? Have you expressed personal love and loyalty to your pastor or to your elders? Maybe you will reply, "No, I'm my own man. I like to keep my options open." Well, God bless you, but understand that God wants to fulfill his purpose through people who are deeply committed to one another.

These men came over to David in battle formation with all kinds of weapons of war. What a tremendous encouragement for him. But not only did they come to David with their weapons and gifts, they also offered him an undivided heart (1 Chron. 12:33). In saying, "We are yours," they implied, "We will use our weapons and gifts to serve you, and we will commit ourselves to you with all our heart."

David received these high-quality new recruits and appointed them as captains of his raiding bands. That is how you should join a local church. It's wise to attend a church for a short time, to assess the anointing of God on it. But once you have sensed that God is moving there and have seen that the work is led by a man after God's heart, you must act. Offer yourself to the church and its leadership, and become fully committed to what God is doing there.

David probably looked out over the vast numbers flocking to him and recalled, "I was cut back once, holed up in a cave with just four hundred untrained men. I worked with them and now they're a powerful fighting force. But God is now adding to us every day, bringing along men of stature. Incredible! It's becoming a great army—like the army of God" (1 Chron. 12:22).

God has his hand on those who obey him. It's hard to be cut back when your contemporaries seem to advance steadily. It's hard to battle through God's disciplines when others seem so free. It's hard to resist the temptation to drop out of the training course halfway through.

Do you want God to use you? Then let him fashion your life. Be patient, and you will find that God's timing is perfect and that you have passed the test. Trust him.

CHAPTER 5

GOD'S MAN SPOILED

If the story of David and Goliath is one of the most glorious in the Bible, the account of David and Bathsheba must be one of the saddest. It's heartbreaking to see a man of God spoiled. The story of David's adultery, although taken from a faraway setting hundreds of years ago, is repeated in our newspapers every day. Indeed, we live in a generation preoccupied with sex, one whose attitude is, "If it feels right, do it." Tragically, this point of view is beginning to infiltrate the church.

Carelessness

What led to David's downfall? Such disasters do not happen in a vacuum. A man like David is not suddenly overcome when he is doing the will of God. A little research reveals a growing carelessness that opened the way.

The story of his adultery pointedly begins "at the time when kings go off to war" (2 Sam. 11:1). It was a time for warfare. Why, then, had David not gone out to battle? He sent Joab to command the army he should have been leading. While the battle was raging, David was resting. Now there is nothing wrong with resting; the Bible encourages us to have times of rest. You can relax and be refreshed. We weren't designed to experience warfare non-stop. But here it clearly states, "It was time for war."

Murray McCheyne, the famous Scottish pastor, said, "Omissions make way for commissions." In other words, sins of omission—things not done—open the door for sins we actively commit. When you are not actively involved in God's purposes, you are susceptible to sin. The best form of defense is to become active in serving the body of Christ. David, at this point, was not. He was just relaxing.

At Gethsemane, Jesus told Peter, James, and John, "Watch and pray so that you will not fall into temptation" (Matt. 26:41), but they fell asleep. When Jesus was arrested they were taken off guard. Peter acted impetuously and cut off someone's ear, and in a panic they all deserted Jesus and fled.

Later Peter followed Jesus from afar. He was mixing with the wrong kind of people when suddenly he was challenged: "You also were with Jesus of Galilee" (Matt 26:69). It was one thing for Peter to be in the company of Jesus and the other disciples, worshiping, healing the sick, enjoying the excitement of the crowds, even walking on water. How he must have loved it all. But now he was alone in the wrong place at the wrong time, and suddenly the challenge was sprung on him: "Surely you are one of them." Peter could not stand that sort of pressure. "I don't know the man!" he declared. The devil picked him off (Matt 26:73,74).

The devil can dislodge the brightest disciple when he drops his guard and relaxes in the wrong situation with the wrong people. Some Christians say, "I have terrible problems with temptation" —but has your carelessness opened the door to that temptation? Don't stay on the fringe of church life. Get in where the action is. The center of God's will is always the safest place to be.

Weakness

David had a weak spot: he was sexually vulnerable. He would accumulate women, taking one wife here and another there. Deuteronomy 17:17 says, "The king...must not take many wives," but David never checked his appetite. He concealed a weakness, one which basically seemed under control, yet had the potential to cause great harm. Sometimes it demanded satisfaction. On one terrible occasion this smoldering character flaw burst into a destructive inferno, so badly scarring David's life that he never fully recovered.

David looked

David's fall began when he looked. You might argue that he could hardly be held responsible for that. He was walking on the rooftop when he glanced down and noticed a woman bathing. But that is where the story should have ended. The king should have turned away immediately.

Only a few decades ago, people would have been shocked at the number of provocative images on display today. Everywhere you go there are tempting sights, but that does not mean that you have to develop an appetite for them. You do not have to let your gaze linger; neither did David.

Under the law Moses received from God, staring at a woman's nakedness was strictly forbidden. Leviticus 18:16 says, "Do not uncover the nakedness of another's wife, for her nakedness belongs to her husband." So if you look at a woman's nakedness, you are stealing from her husband. If she is single, you are still stealing, since she may one day be someone's wife. You are taking what is not yours!

At this point let's stamp out a belief that emerged in the Victorian age, namely that you don't look at nudity because there is something inherently unholy about it. In that era, husbands and wives were actually ashamed of nudity. Some would even go to the lengths of undressing behind screens, or separately entering a specially designed cupboard in order to change their clothes! If believed, these repressive ideas only bring on guilt over human sexuality.

Nowhere does God say that nakedness is impure within marriage. First Corinthians 7:4 says, "The wife's body does not belong to her alone but also to her husband. In the same way, the husband's body does not belong to him alone but also to his wife." Nakedness between them is something wholesome and beautiful. They are free to delight themselves in each another.

The situation outside marriage, however, is quite different. In that case, if you stare, you steal. If you are ever tempted in this way, say to yourself, "She doesn't belong to me. She belongs to another man, and her body is his joy, not mine. I refuse to look."

David soon discovered that the woman was married. Any lingering thoughts of a relationship with her should have terminated there, but they did not. David had been careless, so he was vulnerable. He was not in the battle, not involved in kingdom purposes. He had never dealt with the unchecked appetite in his heart. He allowed his lust to grow and overwhelm him. It all happened so quickly—and to such a man of God!

Who among us can claim to be like David? Remember his magnificent reaction to Saul's hatred; his tears when Saul and Jonathan died. Recall his profound meditations in the Psalms, and you will catch a glimpse of his godly qualities. God loved him. He was unique. For generations to come, God praised people by saying, "He was like David." Here was an extraordinary man—and yet he came crashing down.

David lusted

Lust has terrifying power. Normally, you would ask yourself, "What about the repercussions of this? What if I go ahead and do the thing I shouldn't?" But when lust is fanned into flame, all rational thoughts vanish. Gone are the concerns, "What about my wife, my children, my career, my relationship with God, this woman's husband, her reputation?" These things no longer matter. Lust crashes in like a great tidal wave and sweeps all responsible thinking aside. It fills the emotions and emotions rob the mind of its control. Suddenly you must have satisfaction—now. Lust urges you to live for now. It forces your mind to yield and compels your will to obey. The wave knocks you off your feet. All resolutions to live a godly life are swept aside. David, a man who loved God, was overwhelmed as lust prevailed.

But you need not fall. You have the power to overcome this enemy. God would urge you, "Live a clean life, young man, young woman. I want you free of those unclean habits. I don't want you away from the battle, lying in bed, letting your imagination run wild and then finding yourself overwhelmed with passion." Young Christian couples, what standards are you settling for? Boyfriend, girlfriend—perhaps not engaged, but very fond of one another—what are your standards? How do you conduct yourselves when nobody else is around? Does God approve of what you are doing?

Some people have argued in defense of David. "We mustn't be too hard on David," they say. "He was in a unique position. He was a despotic king in an oriental society. Other kings living at that time wouldn't have thought twice about taking a woman. Bathsheba was not particularly at fault, either. How could she be expected to resist the will of this great monarch? Surely he could have whatever he wanted, so if he wanted Bathsheba, he would have her. We must make allowances for the culture of the day. David was, to some degree, a product of his age, and we must understand that before we judge him for his conduct."

But David was not a mere product of his generation, he was the "man after God's heart." I once read an alarming Gallup survey indicating that 52 percent of regular churchgoers between the ages of thirteen and eighteen did not consider premarital sex wrong. The poll pointed out that this was 10 percent below the national average. But you are not called to be 10 percent better than the world. You are meant to be as different as light and darkness!

God sees the moral landslide that has taken place in the last few decades. He watches as young people are seduced, abused, corrupted. They carry the guilt and shame around with them, yet many young Christians argue, "Everyone's doing it." They accept the world's standard that as soon as they have been going out for a short time they should give rein to their sexual impulses.

"All the other oriental kings did it," say David's defenders. "Everyone else does it"—is that your excuse? Do you adopt worldly standards and merely follow everybody else? Does God's Word tell you that you are free to play around like this? Never!

David was not just another oriental king, a product of his age. He was God's chosen man. All the other kings, in their ungodliness, could do whatever they liked, but David had much higher standards to keep. So have you.

Young men and women, your friends may freely indulge their sexual appetites, but this does not give you license to do the same. Young couples have plenty of opportunities to be together. You may be respected members of your church, trusted to keep God's standards wherever you go. But it is so easy to step into the danger areas.

Young man, you have no right to make demands upon a girl because you have taken her out a few times. Young woman, you have no right to dress provocatively to encourage a boy's advances, and neither of you has the right to ruin each other's future.

Do you really want God to use you? If you do, don't play around. Don't compromise. You cannot easily shake off the accompanying guilt, the sense of failure, and the knowledge that you have laid a landing strip for the devil in your life.

The Bible says, "The righteous are as bold as a lion" (Prov. 28:1). Very often you are not bold, because you are neither righteous nor do you love righteousness. You are, rather, dabbling around on the edge, caught up in the uncleanness of your generation. But God wants you to be as bold as a lion, so cry out to him, "O God, lead me not into temptation, deliver me from evil, help me to be righteous. Give me boldness."

If you are older you must beware of thinking that only young people are vulnerable, that strong passions cease as the years pass. At the time of his adultery, David was about fifty years old!

Maybe you are a man of mature years, going through a dull or difficult period in your marriage. A girl in the office is very warm and understanding. You are flattered that she takes notice of you. You are vulnerable; recognize it and keep away. Determine in your heart, "I will not yield to this temptation. I will not get even remotely involved in such sin. I will not spoil God's plan for me."

Beware of the terrifying power of lust, which like a strong magnet will pull you if you get anywhere near it.

Imagine coming across the story of David and Bathsheba for the first time. You have just read all about David's mighty exploits, his amazing love for Saul and Jonathan, and his promotion to the throne. And now, here he is with another man's wife. It shocks you. How could he do such a thing, this man after God's own heart? How could he wreck the wonderful testimony of his life for the sake of a few moments of pleasure? Surely, if David fell, so can you.

The Bible tells us, "The body is not meant for sexual immorality, but for the Lord.... Flee from sexual immorality. All other sins a man commits are outside his body, but he who sins sexually sins against his own body. Do you not know that your body is a temple of the Holy Spirit, who is in you, whom you have received from God?" (1 Cor. 6:13,18,19). Since God's Holy Spirit lives in you, when you sin against your body, the Spirit is automatically included in your activity. You allow an unholy thing to desecrate the temple of God. You involve a holy and glorious God in your unholy action.

You are a new creation now, so live like it! God is in you, and he will help you. Therefore honor him with your body.

CHAPTER 6

A SINNER FORGIVEN

The story continues; lust is satisfied. Then David says, "Thank you, Bathsheba. Good-bye." Lust is like that. Once satisfied, you have to come back to reality. You have had your fun and now it's time to face real life again—except that you can't just return to life as it was before. Now there are consequences to cope with that will not go away.

David, a mighty monarch who answered to nobody, thought he could get away with his adultery. "You can go now," he said to Bathsheba. He had had his pleasure, so now the poor woman could be dismissed, and that could have been the end of the story. For some people, it often is. A young man gratifies his lust and then wants no further involvement. A young woman recently responded in print, "It seems as though everyone wants your body or your money, but nobody wants you...you are a disposable person to be used and dumped."

Deception
In David's case, the sin was not so easily covered up and forgotten because, to her horror, Bathsheba found she was pregnant. David immediately attempted to cover his tracks. Calling Uriah, her husband, from the battlefield, he encouraged

him to go home and sleep with his wife. But Uriah refused even to go into his house. "There's a battle going on out there," he protested. "How can I possibly go home to my wife and family while my friends are facing warfare?"

Uriah knew that as God's soldier, his place was on the battlefield. He wanted to serve God and his people, as David once had. What a contrast between Uriah's transparent godliness and David's carelessness and deviousness.

Seeing events close in on him, David descended further into the morass of deception. "How can I cover my tracks?" he wondered. "I'll make Uriah drunk. That will weaken his resolve." But still Uriah would not go home.

Eventually, David realized that to conceal his adultery with Bathsheba he had no alternative but to kill her husband. He sent a message to Joab, the army's commander, ordering him to put Uriah in the front line of the battle and then to withdraw from him. One foul action followed another.

I wonder what went through Joab's mind when he received the note. Uriah was listed among David's "mighty men." Joab had to deliberately send this man, one of the elite, handpicked group of thirty, right into a death trap.

I wonder what Joab felt like when he ordered, "Fall back, men," what he thought when he saw Uriah killed and sent David the message, "Uriah is dead." I expect he thought, "My master is known as a godly man—a worship leader and wonderful psalm writer. Now, though, he has done something abominable and will always carry a guilty secret."

David must have found it difficult to ever look Joab in the eye again. If you have sinned greatly, usually somebody knows something about it. You have to live with that. David had to live with it, but essentially he still thought he had covered his tracks.

A whole year passed. David married Bathsheba, and the child was born. "No one else knows exactly what happened," he thought. But Someone did: "The thing that David had done displeased the Lord" (2 Sam. 11:27).

When we first encountered David, he was a man who lived not

for himself, not for others, but for God. But now, in all life's busyness and carelessness, he had forgotten that God, not contemporary morality, sets the standard. He had forgotten that God sees everything. "If I go up to the heavens, you are there; If I make my bed in the depths, you are there.... If I say, 'Surely the darkness will hide me and the light become night around me,' even the darkness will not be dark to you; the night will shine like the day" (Ps. 139:8,11,12).

The Old Testament records the extraordinary story of Jeroboam's wife, who disguised herself and went to see the prophet Ahijah. Before she had even entered the room, Ahijah (who happened to be blind, anyway) said, "Come in, wife of Jeroboam" (1 Kings 14:6). The man was blind, but as God's prophet he still knew what was going on.

You may be able to fool other people into thinking that you are walking uprightly, but you can't hide your ways from God. To him, the darkness is like blazing light. He sees everything, and when he sees sin, he hates it with righteous anger.

God saw David's sin and hated it,but he still loved his servant. If God had not loved him, David would have been destroyed— totally lost. But God had chosen this man and was absolutely committed to him. That's the wonder of it, and that's why the story becomes so painful. For David's own good, God had to uncover the sin so the man could find healing.

David kept his secret for a whole year. Outwardly everything appeared to be going well, but inwardly he was in agony of soul. Psalm 51 in particular records his feelings of alienation from God and his longing to be clean.

No one can play around with sin and still enjoy God. You might sing and dance with everyone else, but inside you will be thinking, "O God, where has the joy gone? Why can't I witness to others any more? I seem to have lost the joy of my salvation." Guilty people cannot rejoice.

Confrontation

God used Nathan, the prophet, to unveil David's heart (2 Sam.

12:1-4). He told the king a story about two men in a city, one rich, the other poor. The rich man has many flocks and herds, but the poor man has nothing except one little ewe lamb. One day, a friend visits the rich man, who, instead of taking a lamb from his numerous flocks, steals the poor man's pet lamb, which he slaughters to prepare a meal for his visitor.

Hearing the story, David, the former shepherd, burned with anger against the rich man and declared his judgment on him. People who have slipped away from a close walk with God are often harsh in their judgment of others. A man who is walking with God is not too quick to condemn people because he knows his own need. But David had become impatient, arrogant, and judgmental. "The man is worthy of death!" While the words still hung in the air, Nathan replied, "You are the man."

Who can imagine the pain and anguish David felt at that moment? Surely, though, the pain was mixed with relief as the foul boil was lanced by the faithful prophet's words, and shame mingled with the security that reality brings in its wake. At last everything was out in the open and before God. "You are the man," said Nathan, but he did not stop there.

"The Lord says, 'I anointed you king over Israel. I delivered you from the hand of Saul. I gave you Israel and Judah. If you had wanted anything else, I would have given it to you. I love you, David. Why did you take what I never gave you?'" God's tender love broke David's heart.

That is God's attitude towards you when you sin. He does not grab a big stick. Rather, he would remind you, "I have anointed you with my Spirit. You are my child and heir. I have delivered you from death, and I have given you my kingdom as your inheritance. You have security, peace, joy, purpose, and so much more. I have gladly given you all these things, and if you had wanted anything else, I would gladly have given you more. I love you. Why, then, do you want to take the things I am not giving you? Why are you reaching out for things I have not given you freedom to touch?"

Forgiveness

If you have ever questioned whether David really was a man after God's heart, look at his response now. The man who sinned knew how to repent and come back to God. There was no hint of self-justification, no argument, no mention of Bathsheba's equal blame. David was broken and no longer tried to hide his sin; he even wrote his confession for all to read. Psalm 51 reveals how deeply he understood the horror of sin and how painfully aware he was that he had offended a holy God.

If you want to know whether you are a child after God's heart, you must note how you respond when your sins are found out. How do you react when your sin is exposed? "It was her fault as much as mine." "Everyone else is doing it." "I couldn't help it." "I found forgiveness last time, so let's get this over with." "If I sin again, I can be forgiven—God is very gracious." These glib responses reveal your desire to get rid of the uncomfortable feeling of guilt, but they show no understanding of the horror of sin. They do not reflect David's attitude—his terrible consciousness that he had offended a holy God.

Let your response be, "O God, you know my sin. I have no argument; what I've been doing is evil in your sight. I know I'm guilty. Please forgive me. I loathe this sin and I want to be free." When you hunger and thirst for righteousness, you will be satisfied. God will cleanse you and set you free.

CHAPTER 7

A HOUSE FOR GOD

David was both warrior and worshiper. He started with a sling and a harp, and he finished with an army and the blueprint for a temple.

All his life he had longed to build a house for God—something majestic and glorious. The thought thrilled him. As it happened, though, God had other ideas. "You are not to build a house for my Name," he told David, "because you have shed much blood on the earth in my sight. But you will have a son who will be a man of peace and rest.... He is the one who will build a house for my Name" (1 Chron. 22:8-10). David's long-cherished plans for building the house of God had to be projected into the future.

Many generations before David, Moses had felt similar yearnings for the house of God. Crossing the Red Sea, he had sung that God would bring his people into Canaan and plant them on the mountain of his inheritance—the place he made for his dwelling, the sanctuary his hands established (Ex. 15:17). Moses' prophetic vision extended through the ages. He realized that God was going to have a city, Zion, and a house in the midst of that city.

Long years after Solomon's reign, the people of Israel backslid and were taken into captivity. The temple fell into ruin and decay. Later the exiles returned, committed to rebuilding it. Haggai, the

59

prophet, encouraged them to build the house for two God-given reasons: that God might take pleasure in it and that he might appear in his glory (Hag. 1:8).

A house to please and honor God

David wanted to have a place where the ark of God and the glory of God might dwell. God's house is built for his pleasure and glory, not to suit our preference.

Of course, the New Testament house of God is a temple made not of bricks and mortar but of "living stones" who are "being built into a spiritual house" (1 Pet. 2:5). We are the living body of Christ, God's house, his "dwelling place" in the Spirit. Some of us need to make changes in our churches, because they hardly seem to be "spiritual houses" at all. Instead, they have become monuments to ritual and formality rather than centers of spiritual activity. A church where God's presence is never felt is a church not worth attending.

Not only does God want to take pleasure in his house, he also wants to appear there in his glory. "I will fill this house with glory," he told the exiles through Haggai. God inhabits the praises of his people. So whenever outsiders come into our church buildings and see us worshiping together, they should be aware of the Lord's presence—not just seeing people being religious, but coming face-to-face with something awesome and wonderful.

In the last few years the church has experienced a little of the glory of God, but he has much more to give us. It should be the desire of all Christians that when they gather with their brothers and sisters week by week they will encounter the glory of God in the house of God. If we exist for him, gathering for any reason other than to meet with him is a waste of time and a total failure to understand our identity. David longed for the house of God, and the Lord Jesus was consumed with zeal for his Father's house. How do you feel about it? Ask yourself, do you love your church or do you merely attend its meetings? Have you progressed beyond a self-centered attitude to your salvation, realizing God has a larger plan for fulfilling his own purpose? Do you realize that you have the privilege of being included in this plan?

The church is the center of all history. Paul Bilheimer, in his book *Destined for the Throne*, gives us a vivid insight into God's perspective of the church. He takes us on an imaginary tour from the conception of a new car to its production. He visualizes offices full of men bent over plans, acres of factories, paint shops, conveyor belts, and vast machines cutting metal, riveting panels, and fitting tires. He sees thousands of people performing innumerable tasks to get the job done. At the end of the day, the only thing that gives sense to everything else is the car that rolls off the end of the assembly line. Without the finished product, all the energy and industry means nothing. Bilheimer concludes, "What is lasting at the end gives you the clue to everything that went before."

God tells us in the Bible that on the last day he will wrap up the heavens and the earth and will cast them aside. As we look at the world and the heavens, at the unfolding of history with its heroes, villains, and countless thousands of unremembered others, what will last forever? What's going to come out at the end? Here is the answer: the bride of Christ! God is seeking a bride, a people to fill a kingdom that will never pass away. This one thing ties all history together. Everything, knowingly or not, is working toward this end.

Many historians say that history teaches us nothing, that it has no pattern or purpose. But the Bible tells us that this is God's creation. The whole thing belongs to him, and when he has finished with it, he will take out his bride—the city of God, the house of God.

A magnificent house

David says, "The house to be built for the Lord should be of great magnificence" (1 Chron. 22:5). That's something to consider. Is your church beginning to be like that? Some churches are experiencing conflict over styles of worship. Deacons march out because someone dared to raise or clap his hands during a rousing hymn. Church councils call meetings because someone was dancing. God is looking for glorious worship, so we should not be content with an out-of-tune piano. We need magnificent instruments played by magnificent musicians, because magnificent things are appropriate for an exceedingly magnificent God. We need the harps as well as the guitars, the trumpets and horns as well as the clarinets and flutes. A vast variety of musical instruments are available to us to express something of the glory of God and the magnificence of his church.

Children do not need to be glued to the television; they can be encouraged to discover their musical talents and use them for the glory of God. And older people can shelve their stereotyped images of the church. They can put behind them the notion that it's dull, rigid, predictable, and totally irrelevant to today's society.

The slipshod and mediocre will not do. In Malachi's day people were sacrificing to God their crippled and diseased animals. "I'd rather you shut the temple doors than bring me unworthy offerings, things you yourselves don't want," God said, adding, "I am a great king. . . and my name is to be feared among the nations" (Mal. 1:14).

When you aim at excellence, people will step into your meetings and experience complete culture shock. They will be assailed by joy, enthusiasm, energy, and exuberant life. And they will say to themselves, "God is here." God is looking for an exceedingly magnificent house, and he will have it. Hallelujah!

A famous house

David told Solomon that God's house would also be "of great fame" (1 Chron. 22:5). Some Christians think that to make the house of God authentic they must keep it small. But God is not looking for a minute remnant through whom he can glorify his name. He wants a huge and famous house. It has been famous in the past. It will be famous again.

Not only will God's house be magnificent and famous, it will also be "of great splendor in the sight of all the nations" (1 Chron. 22:5). God says, "As truly as I live, all the earth shall be filled with the glory of the Lord." How does he fill the earth with his glory? He does not put a golden glow in the sky. Rather, he proclaims his name through his glorious church.

The gospel of the kingdom shall be preached to all nations. It will not be a small evangelistic effort—a few gospel broadcasts and a couple of thousand tracts. In the end times there will be a tremendous missionary thrust. A great wave of supernatural life will send Christians out to the ends of the earth. God's house will be famous and splendid in every land, a glorious international people.

Isaiah 60 says, "I will glorify the house of my glory" (v. 7, NKJV). Then he continued, "The glory of Lebanon shall come to you, the cypress, the pine, and the box tree together, to beautify the place of my sanctuary; and I will make the place of my feet glorious." (v. 13, NKJV). The worldwide church will come together like the glory of Lebanon. Each church will have its own characteristics and abilities. God will reveal himself in our variety, and together we will echo his praise around the world.

"The Sovereign Lord will make righteousness and praise spring up before all nations" (Is. 61:11). God has committed himself to these things. They are not just empty words. "I am the Lord," he says. "In its time I will do this swiftly" (Is. 60:22).

In these last few decades it is as though the Spirit of God has moved into high gear. Worldwide church growth has been of unparalleled proportions. This is true not only numerically, but also in terms of the manifestation of the power and presence of God. The advance of the church in Latin America, Africa, and some parts of southeast Asia has been staggering. God is gathering a glorious international household for himself before he returns in glory.

Have you seen the vision for God's house—its magnificence, fame, and glory? David wanted Solomon to be clear about what he had to build. God wants you to be clear about his objectives in the earth—namely, to glorify his Son by giving him a glorious church from every tribe and nation.

CHAPTER 8

BE STRONG AND COURAGEOUS

Having seen the Architect's plans, how do we turn them into reality?

David did not say to Solomon, "Be nice and laid back," but rather, "Be strong and courageous" (1 Chron. 22:13). The call to build is also a call to battle. The house of God will not build itself. Its construction requires courage, skill, and perseverance. Rugged stones have to be fitted together, beams and pillars positioned to take stress, doors built to give access and to bar intruders, windows put in to give light.

All this has to be done in the face of opposition. The devil will brutally attack church building from the beginning, but building a house has to go ahead on wet and windy days as well as on bright and sunny ones. Your flesh doesn't want to get up early in the morning to pray. It doesn't want to fast. It doesn't want to resist temptation, so you must show your flesh who is boss! The devil will also oppose, tempt, and accuse you, so if you want to build the house, you must be strong.

It's tough to keep going, especially when progress is slow, ugly rumors circulate, and your bones ache with the peculiar weariness that disappointment brings. Having your name dragged through the mud is not fun. You need to take to heart David's words to Solomon, "Do not be afraid or discouraged" (1 Chron. 22:13). Determine in your heart to walk in integrity before God. Live to please him, regardless of what people say. Beware of the logic that whispers, "Better be safe than sorry."

Some of you ministers realize that your jobs may be in jeopardy if you fully preach your vision. It would be easier for you to think, "I must consider my family. My house belongs to the church, and I have no other profession. If I'm thrown out of my job, I don't know how I'll cope. Maybe I'll preach a more palatable message." If you yield to that logic, the battle is lost. God needs fighters who will obey his call to be strong and courageous.

But always remember that the hostility you encounter is not of human origin—even though it comes through people. "Our struggle is not against flesh and blood, but against the rulers, against the authorities, against the powers of this dark world and against the spiritual forces of evil in the heavenly realms" (Eph. 6:12). Unseen forces are desperately trying to resist the great move of God in the world today. That's why Paul echoes David's words to Solomon, "Be strong in the Lord and in his mighty power" (Eph. 6:10). If you are not strong in faith, you will be a loser.

"I will build my church," Jesus said. God's house is the most significant thing in the world today. Indeed, ultimately it is all that matters. World leaders are raised up or removed by God, who has said, "As surely as I live all the earth shall be filled with the glory of the Lord." Whole nations are changed, all because Jesus is building his church.

We are on the edge of God's blessing and revival. Cry out to him, "I want to serve your purpose in my generation. I cannot give myself to something that is not pleasing to you, that will not stand the test of fire. I will be strong. I have only one life to live, and it will soon be over. O God, help me to give myself absolutely to building your house."

Use the resources

"I have taken great pains to provide for the temple of the Lord" (1 Chron. 22:14). David had fought hard in battle, and now he was giving the spoils of those battles to his son to build the temple. He had amassed "a hundred thousand talents of gold, a million talents of silver, quantities of bronze and iron too great to be weighed, and wood and stone" (1 Chron. 22:14).

You can imagine David's words being spoken to you by Jesus: "Now, my child, I have with great pains made available to you everything you need for the house of the Lord." Jesus has conquered death for you, provided at terrible cost everything that you could possibly need to get the job done. "From the fullness of his grace we have all received one blessing after another" (John 1:16). The supply will never run out.

It all seems so difficult, until you realize that Jesus' resources are available to you without limit. No longer do you need to say, "I can't, I'm inadequate" or "Surely we're stretching ourselves too thin." No! There's no limit. However many times you go back for more, there's never any lack of supply. All you need is there on site.

David said further, "You have many workmen: stonecutters, masons and carpenters, as well as men skilled in every kind of work" (1 Chron. 22:15). Not only has God given us a superabundance of grace, he has also given skillful people to work with these resources. You must draw both on God's grace and on the talented people whom God has put with you to teach you how to build his house.

On the one hand, Jesus has given you grace. On the other hand, he has given his whole body, the church, gifted people. "He gave some to be apostles, some to be prophets, some to be evangelists, and some to be pastors and teachers" (Eph. 4:11). He gave skillful people because he wanted them used to build his house.

Pastors, are you encouraging the release of spiritual gifts in your church? Are you using the gifted people God has given you?

Have you asked a gifted and experienced "master builder" if you are building on the right foundation?

Maybe you know that your church is on a good foundation. You are enjoying the family atmosphere, release in worship, and the exercise of spiritual gifts. You are already recovering a New Testament style of church life. But are you evangelizing your town? Or are you essentially inward-looking? Have you called an evangelist to provoke and train you to go out with the gospel?

The church must be built according to God's blueprint—through those whom he has chosen and gifted for this task. If you fail to use them, you are despising the gifts of the ascended Lord.

Apply yourself to the task

"Devote your heart and soul to seeking the Lord your God," (1 Chron. 22:19) David went on. He repeated this exhortation later, as if to emphasize its great importance to success. "And you, my son Solomon, acknowledge the God of your father, and serve him with wholehearted devotion and with a willing mind.... If you seek him, he will be found by you" (1 Chron. 28:9). God had a plan and purpose for Solomon, but he had to apply himself to seek to know God's will.

God has a plan for you. "I know the plans I have for you," declares the Lord, "plans to prosper you and not to harm you, plans to give you a hope and a future. Then you will call upon me and come and pray to me, and I will listen to you. You will seek me and find me when you seek me with all your heart" (Jer. 29:11-13). Note the progression—call, come, pray, seek, and seek with all your heart.

God promised Elijah, "I will send rain on the land," but Elijah still prayed fervently that the rain would come. "Call to me and I will answer you and tell you great and unsearchable things you do not know" (Jer. 33:3). Do you believe this? If you do, you will give yourself to prayer.

So start praying and learn by doing. Pray in large and in small groups. Make room for people who are anointed to pray. Call on

God and see what he will do, and give him no rest until he makes Zion a praise in the earth.

Remember you've been chosen

God had told David, "Solomon your son is the one who will build my house… for I have chosen him to be my son, and I will be his father" (1 Chron. 28:6). David encouraged Solomon by reminding him of that choice. "Consider now, for the Lord has chosen you to build a temple as a sanctuary" (1 Chron. 28:10). Since God had chosen him, he could be bold. So David exhorted his son, "Be strong and courageous, and do the work. Do not be afraid or discouraged, for the Lord God, my God, is with you. He will not fail you or forsake you until all the work for the service of the temple of the Lord is finished" (1 Chron. 28:20).

But just a minute—who was this person God had chosen to build his house? Wasn't he the son of Bathsheba, a woman who should never have appeared in David's history at all? Why should she be honored as the mother of the future king? Who was Solomon that he should be selected? What had he done to deserve such recognition?

Amazing grace! "Where sin increased, grace increased all the more" (Rom. 5:20). When David confessed his sin, God did not simply forgive him but then disqualify him for the future. He forgave completely and thoroughly reinstated David in his purposes.

How many times have you written yourself off? How often have you said, "I give up. Look at my past. Look at the blunders I've made and keep on making. God couldn't possibly use me, he couldn't possibly…could he?" But then, he couldn't possibly have chosen Solomon, could he?

If you are a believer, God has chosen you—not just to barely get by, but to help build his house. It doesn't matter what you have done in the past. If you have come back to him and confessed your sin, he will rejoice over you and thoroughly restore you to his purposes. Glorious, isn't it? God's grace covers your sin and gives you a future beyond your wildest dreams.

Have you seen the vision? Can you say, "O God, I want an expression of your house in my town. I want to see something majestic, famous, and glorious, so that when people walk in they know that this is God's house!"

Have you got the boldness to go for it? God wants you to be strong, to say, "I may lose my reputation, my job, even my home, but Jesus went through much more than that. Whatever it costs, I will proclaim your vision, Lord, and do all I can to fulfill your plan for your house."

Are you using all your resources? There is no reason for you to think, "I can't do this; it's too much for me." Jesus has given you everything you could possibly need for life and godliness (2 Pet. 1:3). You can do all things through Christ who strengthens you (Phil. 4:13). And God has also provided skilled workers. Are they being used and encouraged to bring their God-given gifts and abilities?

Are you applying yourself to the task? How is your prayer life? Taking time to be alone with God is one of the most difficult disciplines for the Christian. If you are finding prayer hard, don't give it up, learn to do it. Grab hold of someone you know who does pray and say, "Can I pray with you sometime, please?" Catch their fervor and apply yourself to prayer.

Remember your call! It is so easy to get discouraged when things get difficult. Then, of all times, you need to remember that you have been chosen by God to build his house. Since he has called you, he cannot fail or desert you. "He who began a good work in you will carry it on to completion until the day of Christ Jesus" (Phil. 1:6).

Do you know why you are building? Are you eagerly waiting for Jesus to return? The house—the church, the bride—is for him. We are being prepared as a bride adorned for her husband.

When Jesus comes again it will not be with a few angels shouting and singing over one small field in Bethlehem. His arrival will be announced by angels over every field, every village, every town, every city in the world. He will not be received by a handful of simple people crouching around his manger making baby noises at him. Every knee will bow and every tongue confess in heaven, on earth, and under the earth. And their united thunderous cry, "Jesus Christ is Lord," will reverberate throughout the universe, to the glory of God the Father.

Let's be strong and courageous and make ready a people prepared for the Lord.

ELIJAH:
A MAN LIKE US

"Elijah was a man just like us."
— James 5:17

CHAPTER 9

NOW ELIJAH. . .

The Western world faces a spiritual dilemma. Millions declare themselves Christians and want the church to baptize their babies, marry their children, and bury their dead. The church adorns such events with respectability, but for everyday life the gospel is regarded as outdated and irrelevant. People do not really want God, but somehow they do not want to let go of him.

Moral standards are on the move. "We're more liberated today," it's claimed. "You have to make room for change." It's rapid change, too! In the sixties, it was unusual for a marriage to end in divorce. Now half of all U.S. marriages fail. A few decades ago, our society would not tolerate abortion. Now statistics show that 30 percent of all pregnancies in the United States end in abortion. In spite of that horrifying statistic, one in four children is now born to an unwed mother. How quickly a nation can change its standards.

A spiritual landslide

Fifty-eight years before Ahab became King of Israel, Solomon was on the throne. His father, David, had fought to establish the kingdom, and Solomon had built up a mighty empire whose splendor became a conversation piece in the highest society. In that fifty-eight years after Solomon, seven kings came and went, each more evil than the one before. By the time Ahab came to power, the nation hardly knew whom they supposedly worshiped.

King Ahab had married a wicked and forceful Baal worshiper named Jezebel. She did not say, "Perhaps I could have a private chapel in your palace. Then I could worship my own god." No, Jezebel was committed to seeing Baal worship dominate the nation.

Ahab, however, was indifferent to spiritual things; that's how he could marry Jezebel in the first place. He mixed his religions. He married an idolator, yet called his children Ahaziah and Jehoram, meaning "Yahweh has grasped" and "Yahweh is exalted," implying, "Even though I've married Jezebel I still want to honor and worship the Lord."

Enter Elijah

Everything about Ahab was vague. By sharp contrast, everything about Elijah was clear-cut. The Bible sometimes gives a few introductory remarks about its heroes, such as how their parents were prepared, or details of birth, or some important childhood events. Elijah, however, seemed to appear from nowhere. We have no record of his past. He just arrived. His prologue is this, "Now Elijah. . ." (1 Kings 17:1). He hadn't been there a minute ago, then he was there, then he was gone again. Eventually he disappeared into heaven. Maybe he was a spaceman or an angel! No, he was flesh and blood; he was vulnerable and had needs. Elijah was a man just like us. And God wants us to become men and women just like him.

Suddenly, standing before King Ahab was a unique figure, totally different from the rest of his generation. Quite how he worked his way through the hierarchy to a meeting with the king must remain a mystery. God alone can arrange such a rendezvous. He told Ananias that Paul was "my chosen instrument to carry my name before. . . kings" (Acts 9:15). Paul didn't know how this would happen, but it happened. David, an obscure shepherd, was brought before King Saul, and Moses confronted mighty Pharaoh. God is well able to raise people out of obscurity and to give them a voice before the nation's leaders. Doubtless he will do so again.

Standing before God

Elijah did not mince words when he encountered the king. "As the Lord, the God of Israel lives, before whom I stand, surely there shall be neither dew nor rain these years, except by my word" (1 Kings 17:1, NASB). Elijah spoke with all the authority of one who came from the presence of God, so that in meeting Elijah, Ahab was really being confronted by God. Pharoah had a similar experience when he met Moses.

The backslidden western world waits to be confronted by Christians who have come from the presence of God with a clear, uncompromising message. So often we hope we can impress people in the world by being more like them, employing their methods. Our real need, though, is for Christians who know God intimately and can powerfully and authoritatively declare his word because they live before him.

Elijah's proud boast was that he stood before God. The world too often detects our uncertainties. We do not sound like people who genuinely know God. Our message often lacks credibility because it lacks assurance. We seem to carry our doubts into the battlefield. We even fear to be called narrow-minded or opinionated, forgetting that we serve a narrow-minded God who commands all men everywhere to repent. He leaves no room for negotiation and is willing to back an uncompromising prophet with signs and wonders to prove his authenticity. In this case, he decreed that there would be no rain until Elijah said so.

Living in the world

Although Elijah lived before God, he was not cut off from his society. Later in the story we shall meet Obadiah, who had a rather different story. We are told that "Obadiah was a devout believer in the Lord" (1 Kings 18:3). Here was a man who genuinely knew and feared God, but his master was not so much God as Ahab. As Ahab's servant, he made no meaningful impact on his nation. Beware the danger of being so enveloped within the system that you are compromised and cannot make a real impact on it.

In contrast, a hundred prophets who were contemporaries of Elijah withdrew completely. They all hid themselves away, and also became totally ineffective.

A monastic group called "The Inclusi" did their best to forsake the world by shutting themselves in a little monastery. One day someone who was feeding them through the slit windows asked, "Are you alive?" And the answer came back, "I believe I am dead to the world." If we become like that, no one will even know that we exist. By all means be dead to the world's values, but still make sure your presence is felt!

Elijah said, "I stand before God," but he was also totally involved with what was happening in his nation. As he confronted Ahab he was saying, in effect, "You cannot shake me off or ignore me. I will be seen and heard!"

Jesus didn't hide himself away from the crowds. He put himself where it really counted, earning the title "friend of sinners," yet remaining both untouched by their sin and unwilling to adjust his message to accommodate them.

"Standing before the Lord" has all kinds of implications for the way you behave in your marriage, your friendships, your business affairs, your school. You might find yourself saying, "No, I can't enter into that transaction," or "I will not get engaged to you." When the response comes, "Why not?" you answer, "Because I stand before the Lord, and his will affects my decisions." If some wonder why you don't withdraw from the world and hide out in a monastery somewhere, let them know you intend to live a life honoring God wherever he has put you— in school, at your job, or wherever. Your example will confront people with the reality that God desires all of us to honor him.

The Lord is saddened to see Christians hiding their testimony and compromising their faith. How will the lost ever get the chance to hear the gospel? God wants us to create situations in which we can vindicate his name. Be where the people are, yet be totally distinctive. You will make mistakes, but you must trust God to give you boldness, courage, and wisdom to handle increasingly provocative situations.

Adopting God's perspective

Elijah stood both before the Lord and with the Lord. He developed a God-centered perspective on what was happening in his nation. He saw through God's eyes, felt through God's heart, and proclaimed God's word of judgment on the land, "There will be neither dew nor rain in the next few years except at my word" (1 Kings 17:1).

The prophet was not speaking off the top of his head. He knew that God had chosen the Israelites "above all the nations" (Deut. 10:15) and had promised them a land of their own—a fertile land, not one like Egypt, where they had to use treadmills to get water out of the Nile in order to prevent the land from drying up.

"Love and serve me," the Lord had said, "and I will send rain on your land in its season, both autumn and spring rains, so that you may gather in your grain, new wine and oil" (Deut. 11:13,14). But then Moses had warned the people that if they sought other gods, "then the Lord's anger will burn against you, and he will shut the heavens so that it will not rain and the ground will yield no produce, and you will soon perish from the good land" (Deut. 11:17).

So when Elijah told Ahab, "The rain is going to stop," he was not thinking to himself, "How can I impress the people? I know. I'll pray that God will stop the rain." Not at all! He remembered that the Lord had said, "Follow me and I'll bless you with rain, but go after other gods and the rain will stop." Since the people had decided to go after Baal, Elijah simply prayed, "God, fulfill your word."

That was an amazing prayer: Elijah actually asked God to devastate the nation, to bring it crashing down. "O God, deal with this generation," he was saying. "Bring it to its knees. Shut up the heavens. Bring chaos." I wonder how long it took him to find the passion and courage to pray that. An equivalent modern-day prayer might be, "O God, stop the oil supply. Let there be huge lines at the gas pumps and terrible problems heating homes and fueling businesses. Bring the nation's economy to a standstill."

To pray a prayer of that magnitude you have to be standing very close to God. This was not a normal request like, "Lord, bless us on Sunday. Impress people by the lively meetings we have." Elijah had a passion for God's glory and for his people. "I want to serve God's purposes in my generation," he was saying. "Whatever God wants me to do, I want to do—whatever it costs."

Elijah was committed to the vindication of God's name. As an Israelite, he would be personally affected by the consequences of his prayer. He was no angel who could deliver his message and then retreat to another sphere. He was a man just like us.

CHAPTER 10

FAITH ON TRIAL

As soon as Elijah had delivered his message to the king, God told him to go and hide in the Kerith Ravine. So Elijah "did what the Lord had told him" (1 Kings 17:5). It was on God's instruction that he had confronted Ahab in the first place. Now there was a new word from the Lord: "Go." So Elijah went.

One hundred percent obedience

He did not question or murmur against the instruction. He didn't say, "What, Lord? The ravine? You've commanded the ravens to feed me? But Lord, haven't you ever read Leviticus 11:13-15? Look, here it is. It says, 'These are the birds you are to detest. . . any kind of raven.' It's an unclean bird, Lord. And how on earth are they going to feed me anyway? The whole idea's ludicrous. And if I do eventually decide to go, I'll be taking a sandwich along—and some fruit, and maybe a handful of pretzels, a few cookies, and something cold to drink. . . ."

No. We hear nothing of this. God spoke, and there was no protest from his servant. Elijah accepted the word without question—a God-honoring characteristic often seen in the prophet's story.

Obedience underlies power

Elijah's obedience was one of the keys to his dynamic prayer life. The Bible says, "The prayer of a righteous man is powerful and effective" (James 5:16). God listens to those who listen to him. When you take seriously what God says to you, you can expect God to take seriously what you say to him. Jesus said, "If you remain in me and my words remain in you, ask whatever you wish, and it will be given you" (John 15:7). Does this mean that God answers those who have succeeded in memorizing lots of Bible texts? No. That's a good discipline, but Jesus is referring to a lifestyle that is built upon his word like a house is built on rock.

When God spoke, Elijah acted and, later in the story, Elijah spoke and God acted. What a wonderful relationship! As you increasingly trust and obey God's word you will discover an increasing level of fellowship with him, and a growing experience of his power.

Obedience to strange requests

God's command to Elijah was unusual, but the prophet still obeyed it. Jesus gave the disciples some unusual instructions. "Go to the lake," he told Peter, "and throw out your line. Take the first fish you catch; open its mouth and you will find a four-drachma coin" (Matt. 17:27). And, "Go and prepare the Passover. As you enter the city you will meet a man with a jar of water. Follow him and he will lead you to the house where we will be eating" (Luke 22:8-10). "Throw your net on the right side of the boat and you will find some fish there" (John 21:6).

Why did Jesus instruct his disciples to do such strange things? He wanted to develop their obedience. He wanted them to live not by their own reason and wisdom but by his word. The more they acted on Jesus' word, the more they trusted it. The more they trusted it, the more they acted on it. Jesus' mother learned this lesson, too. "Do whatever he tells you," (John 2:5) she told the servants at the wedding in Cana, and their obedience brought about a miracle.

Sometimes God's word to us is unusual. "Love your enemies

and pray for those who persecute you" (Matt. 5:44). "Give, and it will be given to you" (Luke 6:38). "Rejoice in the Lord always" (Phil. 4:4). Sometimes God may ask us to do odd things. He's watching to see our reaction to his word. Will it be, "That's illogical, Lord. It doesn't make sense, so I won't do it"? Or will it be, "I don't understand the reasoning behind this, but because you say so, I will let down the nets" (Luke 5:5)? Only when you reach out with Peter's faith and obedience will you enjoy the miraculous blessing.

Present obedience to past revelation

"I've ordered the ravens to feed you there," God told Elijah (1 Kings 17:4). First comes the commandment, then the promise. We often want the promise fulfilled before we obey the naked command to go. We ask God to provide "here" before we go so we don't wind up vulnerable and empty-handed. But God had commanded the ravens to feed Elijah "there," at the brook Kerith. God will prove his faithfulness in providng if we will demonstrate our faithfulness by being at the appointed place. Every day there was food, just as there had been when the Israelites trusted God for the manna from heaven. He truly is Jehovah Jireh to all who trust him, whether it be an individual or a whole nation.

Perhaps God is calling you, for example, to move and help plant a new church elsewhere. Immediately questions arise. "Can I afford to live there? What about my children's education? It's a tough area," to which God replies, "The ravens will be there. You go and prove me."

Miracles come when you obey. I have received letters from people saying, "God told me to do this. I trusted him and since then amazing things have happened." But these people had to move out from here to there—to the place where God sent the ravens.

The faith to stay

It's exciting to go in faith, trusting in God's promises and reaching out into something new. It's harder to sustain that faith when pressures develop, as Elijah discovered when the brook Kerith began to dry up.

Imagine the devil whispering to him, "Elijah, have you noticed that the drought is beginning to affect the water level of the brook? Be sensible. You know you can't live without water. I'd go now if I were you; otherwise the ravens will not so much be feeding you as feeding from you."

Sometimes we go "there" in faith, only to find that something "there" begins to dry up. "Lord," we protest, "didn't you tell me to go there in the first place? And didn't I obey you? So what's happening? The water's nearly gone. Where are you in this?" And when there's no answer from God, we start to reason with ourselves. "Yes, God did bring me here, but it's too hard for me now. I don't know how much more of this situation I can stand. This house, this job, this project, this home life, this pressure— I don't think I can take it any more." And we make plans to move on.

That's what many people today do. When things get difficult, they drop out. "I can't stand this any longer," they say. "It's time to leave. I'm gone." But for the Christian who has received no word from God, leaving is dropping out. You may say, "I can't stand this another day," but God knows exactly how many more days you can stand. And he is watching you to see if you have the faith to stay where he sent you even when the brook is drying up. Beware of putting your faith in the water and not in the word of God.

Faith, not sight

The word that Elijah longed to hear came at the last moment, the day the brook actually dried up. "Go at once to Zarephath. . . . I have commanded a widow in that place to supply you with food" (1 Kings 17:9). The prophet must have sighed with relief and thought, "Terrific! A home at last. I would have preferred the offer of a more luxurious house, but at least I will have some human company. You don't get much fellowship with a raven: 'Beautiful day isn't it, ravens?' 'Caw. Caw.' 'What's for lunch today?' 'Caw.' 'What do you think about the political situation of the nation?' 'Caw. Caw. Caw.' Oh, boy! Am I looking forward to some intelligent conversation. I bet she's excited, too. God has told her she's going to have a prophet to come visit. I can see her now, basting the roast, baking the cakes—I can almost smell the cooking. Oh, joy!"

When Elijah arrived at Zarephath, he met a woman. "Is this the widow?" he must have thought. "She's expecting me, so I'd better find the right password. I wonder what it is? Something to do with food, surely. As soon as I say 'eat' or 'drink' she'll know that I'm the one she's waiting for.

"Excuse me, ma'am. Can you give me some water and bread, please?" But the widow didn't suddenly exclaim, "Oh, so you're the prophet!" and then shake him warmly by the hand. She said, "I don't have any bread—only a handful of flour in a jar and a little oil in a jug. I am gathering a few sticks to take home and make a meal for myself and my son, that we may eat it—and die" (1 Kings 17:12). What a welcome.

How did Elijah react? Did he say to himself, "Lord, I thought you said you had commanded a widow to feed me! Well she doesn't know anything about it, and she hasn't exactly got an abundant supply of food. Your plans have all gone wrong. It's a hopeless mess. We'll manage one scanty meal, and then it's curtains for all of us!"

No. Elijah's response was magnificent. He did not allow his dilemma to damage his faith. Instead he took note that the woman said her last meal was for herself and her son. There was no husband. She was a widow, indeed, and God had promised a widow. Although the situation was outwardly bleak, Elijah believed he was still on course, and he sustained his walk of faith by telling her, "Go home and do as you have said. But first make a small cake of bread and bring it to me, and then make something for yourself and your son" (1 Kings 17:13).

How often we give up when we are actually still on course. How often we think, "Oh, God, you told me. . . and it's not working. What's gone wrong?" Moses probably thought that. God had told him, "I am sending you to Pharaoh to bring my people the Israelites out of Egypt" (Ex. 3:10). But when Moses tried to get the people out, he met not with enthusiasm, but with opposition. God had told Moses that Pharaoh would resist for a while, but Moses must have assumed that when Pharaoh had seen a couple of miracles, he would be bound to let the people go. This was not the case. In fact, things got so bad that Moses protested to God, "O Lord, why have you brought trouble upon this people? Is this why you sent me? Ever since I went to Pharaoh to speak in your name, he has brought trouble upon this people, and you have not rescued your people at all" (Ex. 5:22,23).

Do you feel like that about your situation? Well, did God tell you things would happen immediately, or does his plan need time to unfold? Are you walking by faith or by sight? It's easy to believe what you see, but "faith is being sure of what we hope for and certain of what we do not see" (Heb. 11:1).

Elijah believed that God would provide his needs through this widow, so he did not yield to the thought, "This is a hopeless mess." Rather, he resisted unbelief and told the woman not to fear. Then, because he remained in faith, his prophetic gift began to flow: "The jar of flour will not be used up and the jug of oil will not run dry until the day the Lord gives rain on the land" (1 Kings 17:14). Elijah's faith and prophetic word released the woman into faith, too. She provided for him until the rain came— just as God had said she would.

Have faith to see that God is committed to doing what he promised. Don't drop out because of disappointments and delays. God wants to give you a breakthrough. Keep believing for his provision—for your husband, your wife, your children, your parents, your church, even yourself. There will be no running out of resources. Hold your ground. Keep believing, move out increasingly into the supernatural, and rejoice when God provides everything that he has promised.

CHAPTER 11

INTO THE CRUCIBLE

I wonder if Elijah opened his Bible dictionary and looked up Zarephath to find out the Hebrew derivation. If he had, he would have discovered that Zarephath means "crucible" or "place of testing." As he strolled around the neighborhood, I don't suppose he gave the name of the town a second thought. After all, he had won a great battle of faith, and God was supplying the food he had promised. Things were beginning to settle down. Little did he know that God was about to heat them up—in the crucible.

Suddenly there was a crisis: the widow's son died. She had already lost her husband, and now even her son was being snatched from her. In her agony of soul she turned on Elijah and blamed him. "What do you have against me, man of God? Did you come to remind me of my sin and kill my son?" (1 Kings 17:18). People who are in heartbreaking situations often lash out, saying, "This is God's judgment on my life." And Elijah, who had brought faith, blessing, and godliness into the woman's home, found himself facing tragedy and hostility.

Identification

The prophet did not retaliate. He did not rebuke her for her anger, and neither did he say, "Well, I'm very sorry to hear about your son. But, you understand, I'm concerned about the state of the nation. I really haven't got time to deal with issues of lesser importance." He didn't say, "I'm sorry about your problem. Naturally I'll pray about it." Elijah's response was amazing. He said, "Give me your son" (1 Kings 17:19) —"give your problem to me." Later Elijah took a national problem onto his shoulders when he stood on Mount Carmel and said to the Israelites, "Come here to me" (1 Kings 18:30). "I'll carry the weight for you. Come to me."

If I had been prepared to help the widow, I probably would have asked her to lay her son on the sofa or on his own bed. After all, he was dead, and although I might have been willing to pray, I would not have wanted to identify so wholeheartedly with the crisis and make it my own. But Elijah didn't respond this way. He picked up the boy, carried him upstairs, and put him on the bed where he himself slept. "I will not shrug off your problem," he implied. "I'll identify with it. I'll take it on myself. I'll carry it for you."

Then Elijah "stretched himself out on the boy three times and cried to the Lord" (1 Kings 17:21). There was probably no significance in the number of times the prophet lay on the boy. Later, on Mount Carmel, Elijah told his servant seven times to check the sky for rain. There is unlikely to be any significance to this number either. The fact is that on both occasions Elijah prayed as long as it was necessary for God to do the work. "No answer yet," he thought. "I won't let go of this. I'll just keep on interceding until God answers. I will take the responsibility." And in secret God fashioned his servant for his future public ministry. The popular notion is that maturity comes with age. Not true: you get old with age. Maturity comes with the acceptance of responsibility.

We often want to be in the limelight. "Isn't it about time you used me in a more public way?" we protest to God. "My ministry is not being adequately recognized." But what have we proved about ourselves secretly? What have we done that no one but

God and a widow know about? While the national battle rages on, God wants to hide us away like Elijah and prepare us in humble surroundings, far away from the big platform.

God is looking for people who will reach out where others are hurting, people who will say, "I'm here to help you. Give your burden to me." Maybe he wants you to get to know one individual, someone who just can't cope with life. How do you react to that? Will you say, "Yes, I'll do it; give me the problem; I'll hold it; I'll give myself to it"? Are you sure? Can you put a corpse on your bed?

If we can't stay with God in the secret battles, how can we expect God to trust us in the more public ones? If you want to be used mightily by God, you must be willing to let him hide you away in his quiver, willing to let him sharpen you through times of testing, willing to let him polish into you the lessons he wants you to learn. If you will allow God to deal with you like this, there will come a day when he declares, "That's enough training. I'm taking you out. I'm putting you into my bow and giving you the visibility you can now handle."

Vindication

We next read, "The Lord heard Elijah's cry, and the boy's life returned to him, and he lived" (1 Kings 17:22). It's easy to be involved in Christian activity for the praise of men, but God looks at the things that remain secrets between him and us. So when Jesus saw a poor widow throw two small copper coins into the collection box, he said, "That's genuine sacrifice." God's vindication is the only vindication worth having.

Imagine Elijah's joy as he gave the boy back to his mother. What rejoicing must have filled the house that night! God vindicated Elijah because of his faith and obedience. In contrast, King Saul wanted vindication to come cheaply. He despised the amazing privilege that he had been given and threw away his right to rule. But when Samuel told him, "The Lord has torn the kingdom of Israel from you today," (1 Sam. 15:28) Saul replied, "I have sinned. But please honor me before the elders of my people and before Israel" (1 Sam. 15:30). Yes, there was a faint acknowledgement of wrong, but no sign of true repentance. Saul did not say, "I'm going to fast and pray and get right with God." All he was concerned about was his reputation. "Stay with me, Samuel. You're the national prophet. Stay with me. Vindicate me before men."

"How can you believe," said Jesus to the Pharisees, "if you accept praise from one another, yet make no effort to obtain the praise that comes from the only God?" (John 5:44). You will never develop genuine faith if you have that attitude. Elijah was able to say, "You know about my secret devotion. You know I stand before you." And the God who saw what Elijah had done in secret rewarded him openly. There are no short cuts to being useful to God. Even Jesus had the testimony that he learned obedience through his sufferings (Heb. 5:8). Will you embrace God's training and testing? Only God knows what is ahead for you. In Elijah's case, the training was for a ministry that would affect the whole nation.

Maybe God is taking you through severe trials and pressures. Maybe you wonder if you can take much more of it. Maybe you don't even really know what's happening to you. Remember Elijah: God was preparing him for a huge stage appearance on Mount Carmel, a historical event comparable with the fall of Jericho or the parting of the Red Sea. God does not want to see you run away as soon as things begin to get difficult. He wants you to be diligent, to break through, to develop some spiritual muscle. You have a great calling. Receive God's hidden preparation. The day will come when you will call for the fire of God and he will vindicate you fully.

CHAPTER 12

THE TROUBLER
OF ISRAEL

Well away from the public eye, Elijah submitted to God's training and proved that the Lord was able to perform miracles. Now the prophet emerged from hiding, confronted the nation of Israel, and prepared for the display of God's mighty power.

"Go tell your master, 'Elijah is here,'" the prophet told the reluctant Obadiah (1 Kings 18:8). When Ahab arrived there was a distinct chill in the air. "Is that you, you troubler of Israel?" he asked (1 Kings 18:17). No sign of repentance, no compassion for the starving poor in the land. Ahab was preoccupied with his animals, trying to keep them nourished during the famine (1 Kings 18:5).

Elijah was viewed as a troublemaker. He was thought to be the source of the problem! Jeremiah was similarly hated by his contemporaries. "If you are a national prophet..." they said, "...you should be encouraging us, not telling us to repent and surrender to the Babylonians. This is treachery. You're a traitor to your own nation." And they imprisoned him. (See Jer. 38:1-6.)

Prophets from Amos to John the Baptist experienced the pain of rejection from God's people. For two years Paul taught quite freely in Ephesus. Then, when his message began to threaten vested economic interests, his very life was in danger! (Acts 19:10-41). The Pharisees accused Jesus of stirring up people all over Judea through his teaching (Luke 23:5). John Wesley suffered persecution from both the crowds and religious leaders. Many years passed before he was recognized and honored as a great man of God. Throughout church history, from Bible times onward, prophets have raised their voices only to be labeled "troublemakers."

You troublemaker!

If you are doing your job properly, you will at some time or another be seen as a troublemaker. It's inevitable, because you are identifying with a God who has a rebel world on his hands. As you walk through it, you will upset it. Though to some people you will be "the fragrance of life," to others you will be "the smell of death" (2 Cor. 2:16). So don't think it strange when you experience backlash. Believers before you have endured it and triumphed, Elijah among them.

Do not deliberately make trouble by being obnoxious, but do not live passively in an attempt to avoid righteous conflict. In order for salt to affect society, it has to be scattered where the action is. Get involved—get elected to the city council, PTA leadership, or student government—and stand for righteousness.

God called Jeremiah when he was young, saying, "Before you were born I set you apart; I appointed you as a prophet. . . . Stand up and say to them whatever I command you. They will fight against you but will not overcome you, for I am with you and will rescue you" (Jer. 1:5,17,19).

It was a hard calling for a sensitive man. True, Jeremiah brought some wonderful new covenant promises, but at the outset of his ministry he was told that he would encounter opposition. More than once he cried to God, "Enough is enough. I don't want to prophesy any more. Every time I speak, I get into hot water. It's time you found me another job. Here's my resignation."

I once did that. I was having a tough time in my first pastorate. Growing numbers were being filled with the Holy Spirit, while others were antagonistic. For several years the battle went on. Even the elders were at loggerheads. "When will the break-through come?" I cried. "How can God possibly bless us when there's so much tension among the leadership? I cannot go forward. It's time to quit." I wrote out my letter of resignation and when I had finished it, God said, "Hmm. . . . very nice. Now throw it away."

When you know that you are in the will of God, where else can you run? The barriers to progress may be there—the Red Seas, the Jordan Rivers, the walls of Jericho—but you have no choice except to push on. If you have definitely been sent by God and you maintain your faith, the breakthrough must come!

Compassionate troublemakers

"No more," said Jeremiah; and then the word of God so consumed him that he had to speak (Jer. 20:9). The prophet did not observe his nation from a distance. He cared passionately for it. The book of Lamentations tells us that he wept rivers of tears over it (3:48). He hated the message he had to bring, but it was God's word for the people. In reality the man who was branded a traitor loved his nation more than anyone else.

True prophets not only speak penetrating words, they grieve. As Jesus "approached Jerusalem and saw the city, he wept over it" (Luke 19:41). Then he pronounced God's judgment on it. "Your enemies. . . will dash you to the ground, you and the children within your walls. They will not leave one stone on another, because you did not recognize the time of God's coming to you" (Luke 19:43,44). His prophecy was fulfilled—but he wept as he gave it. May God deliver us from cold-hearted prophets.

God hates wickedness and we cannot condone it; but as we bring his word, we must do so with deep compassion. It is said that as vast crowds gathered to hear George Whitefield (perhaps the greatest evangelist Britain has ever known), those standing at the front felt his tears fall upon them as he preached and gave his uncompromising call to repentance.

Jesus felt deeply for the harassed, helpless crowds, like sheep without a shepherd. What does he think about our generation, in which children are abused by members of their own families, ravaged before they ever know anything of life? Today sin is learned at an early age, and one generation quickly teaches the next.

Today's children are being steadily engulfed by the most appalling practices. In films they see Superman and James Bond taking their girlfriends to bed, and learn to regard such behavior as a perfectly natural part of life. "Sex is easy—something to experience as soon as possible."

It has been calculated that in the U.S., in the course of one year, children under ten can see over 9,000 illicit sex acts on television; American adults can watch over twice that number. But the characters in these films never express remorse or anguish. No one ever says, "What have I done?" Nobody mentions the cost involved. No one says, "Look, sex without marriage affects you emotionally, psychologically, economically, medically, and spiritually." No one says, "There is no such thing as free sex. You are deeply involved. It ruins you. It breaks your heart and it costs you everything." No one is seen paying the price.

Society teaches us that anything done privately between two consenting adults is acceptable. "You can't bring your Christian values into what we do in private," people say. "We're consenting adults, and what we do behind closed doors is none of your business. How dare you seek to moralize over us! We're just more liberated than you. It's free sex!"

But if sex is free, why is society paying such a price? Again, because there is no such thing as free sex. What two consenting adults do in private involves us all. Tragically, today's children are being led to believe that there's no cost involved. The modern-day message that pounds into their lives is this: "It's easy. It's free. If you feel like it, go ahead and do it."

With such a moral landslide in our world you will be tempted to give up, to think, "I can't do much. Who am I to confront that situation anyway? It's just too hard." But don't give up. Elijah refused to compromise his message or waive his responsibility. Singlehandedly he fought to bring a nation back to God.

The church today is beginning to be renewed and restored. We're living in exciting times—but we must not keep our spiritual renewal to ourselves. We are being freshly equipped to fulfill a great task that will take us beyond the four walls of our buildings. But we must be sure of this, that as we begin to speak up for righteousness, we shall be seen as "troublers of Israel."

Whitefield and Wesley were mocked and treated shamefully when they first raised their voices in England, but God stood by them and vindicated their message until a nation was transformed. Before they were ever accepted as saviors, though, they were hated as troublemakers.

Jesus said, "You will be hated by all nations because of me" (Matt 24:9). Why? Because "this gospel of the kingdom shall be preached in the whole world for a witness to all the nations" before the end comes (Matt. 24:14).

Wherever the gospel is preached, two responses will be found: rejoicing and hatred, acceptance and refusal, delight and denunciation.

Let's go and trouble the nations!

CHAPTER 13

THE TROUBLE
WITH TOLERATION

Ahab was a pathetic figure. A spineless individual, he sat on the fence while Jezebel steamrolled the nation into Baal worship and all the wickedness that went with it.

The intrigue that led to the theft of Naboth's vineyard was typical of their relationship. Ahab wanted it as a vegetable garden, but Naboth was not prepared to let go. He was quite within his rights to refuse, but Ahab could not face being turned down. Sullen and angry, he went home, refused his food, lay on his bed and sulked (1 Kings 21:4). That's how his wife found him—whimpering and whining. No wonder she retorted, "Is this how you act as king over Israel?" (1 Kings 21:7).

Jezebel took over the situation, and Ahab made no protest. "Get up and eat! Cheer up. I'll get you the vineyard" (1 Kings 21:7). Then she rushed off to plot against Naboth, had him killed, and returned to Ahab with the news that he could go and claim the vineyard. The king asked no questions, but simply took up his latest acquisition.

You tolerate

Ahab did not challenge Jezebel. His great sin was that he

tolerated her. In the Old Testament, the people of Israel were clearly instructed to destroy Baal worship.

"When the Lord God brings you into the land. . . and drives out before you many nations. . . then you must destroy them totally. Make no treaty with them and show them no mercy" (Deut. 7:1,2). So when the Israelites entered the Promised Land, they were not only gaining an inheritance, they were executing God's judgment on the peoples and their evil religions.

The tragedy came when the Israelites disobeyed this clear-cut command. Psalm 106:34-37 outlines the terrible downward spiral:

1. They did not destroy the peoples.
2. They mingled with the nations and adopted their customs.
3. They worshiped their idols, which became a snare to them.
4. They sacrificed their children to demons.

The Israelites were meant to be God's special people, those who reflected his holiness. Instead, they ended up doing the same foul things as the nations around them. No wonder the Lord was angry with them. No wonder he allowed their enemies to oppress them. He wanted to bless them, but they acted as if they did not belong to him. They tolerated and then adopted the standards they were meant to hate.

Ahab was typical of Israel's failure in that he married and tolerated Jezebel. He totally compromised the nation's unique calling. Elijah, in stark contrast to Ahab, stood in total opposition to the prophets of Baal and invited a showdown that would vindicate the true God of Israel. He hated the compromise that was crippling the nation. He could not tolerate the woman Jezebel.

Strangely, we find Jesus echoing the same sentiments in the New Testament. When sending a letter to the church at Thyatira (Rev. 2:20), he first warmly encouraged them and then added, "I have something against you." How dreadful that the Savior should have something against his church! What could it be? "You tolerate that woman Jezebel." There was sin in the church and it was not being dealt with. Under the new covenant, then,

Christians are called upon to display the same ruthlessness in their hatred of sin as did Elijah.

Jesus said, "If your right eye causes you to sin, gouge it out and throw it away. . . . And if your right hand causes you to sin, cut it off and throw it away" (Matt. 5:29,30). We must not tolerate sin.

You tolerate what you say

"What about your swearing habit?" Jesus would ask some Christians. You reply, "Oh, that's just me. Sometimes I lose my temper. I suppose I'll come to grips with it one day." You excuse yourself so easily, but where is your conscience? How can you continue to go to meetings, singing the praises of Jesus with the same mouth you used to curse those whom he loves?

"What about your gossip?" he would ask others. You say, "Well, that's just me. I don't mean any harm." But whether you mean harm or not, God is not honored by your conversation. He is not blessed by hearing you tear someone's life to shreds with your words. He has something against you.

You tolerate what you see

You should not be watching some of those television programs or reading suggestive books and magazines. You're looking at the wrong sort of pictures. You know it's wrong, yet you tolerate it.

You tolerate what you touch

When you fail to be ruthless in dealing with these issues they begin to undermine your Christian standards. Fantasy gives way to action.

You go to bed at night and dwell on your imagination. You say, "Well, it's not doing any harm. It's not affecting anyone else." And you succumb to temptation. You don't put up any fight at all. You totally fail to say, "This is no way for a child of God to act. My body is the temple of the Holy Spirit. My standards are higher than this. I will not do it."

Jesus is saying to many Christian young couples, "I have

something against you." You are tolerating the things that you are doing with your hands when no one's looking. You are going too far. You have allowed the spirit of this age to creep into your relationship before you are married. Recognize who you are. Do not compromise. Set your hearts on purity.

You tolerate wrong relationships

Some believers are flirting outside marriage. "My marriage is not what it used to be," they say. "That man, that woman was very sensitive to me. We get on well together." You're not being clear-cut. You're not saying, "None of that." You're tolerating it, enjoying the attention, and fantasizing about a relationship which is acceptable to society but forbidden by Scripture.

Families are falling apart because married couples are tolerating second best. "Our relationship is not where it should be," they say. "The spark disappeared ages ago. We don't love each other any more, and we've given up trying to fan the flame. Other people are in the same boat. We're content just to survive for the sake of the children."

But isn't Christian marriage meant to reflect the beautiful and intimate relationship between Christ and the church? If you are having difficulties, shouldn't you be on your faces before God, pleading for his help? Shouldn't you be seeking the counsel of others? Shouldn't you be humbling yourselves, repenting, and battling with all your hearts to get your marriage back on track?

You tolerate your weekday conduct

There are Christians who cheat in their place of work—bosses who run their businesses poorly and employees who are lax about their timekeeping and casual about their output. They are not necessarily evil; they may not be plotters of wickedness as Jezebel was. But, like Ahab, they tolerate compromise and turn a blind eye.

You tolerate things in your church

"If we touch that situation, it will blow up in our faces," say some church leaders who are caught in a predicament. "We dare not stop him from doing that. There would be an almighty uproar. Let's keep quiet and hope that something changes." So nothing is said, and the longer the silence reigns, the further the church drifts.

You tolerate things in your nation

"Church," says Jesus, "I have this against you. You are tolerating things in your nation. Like weak, uncommitted Ahab, you are allowing the tide to carry you along. I want you to turn and confront wickedness, to speak against it, to be strong by my grace and stop the waves of evil from eroding your lives."

What are you tolerating?

Jesus would say to many Christians today, "I love you. I'm with you. I want you to reflect my glory—but I have something against you. You are tolerating things that my Word forbids." How far will you go to establish righteousness in your life? To what extent do you want God to bless and use you?

"Seize the prophets of Baal," said Elijah. "Don't let anyone get away!" Then he slaughtered them all. He was radical. He showed no mercy. He would not tolerate anything that compromised the high standards of God. He did what God had wanted the Israelites to do centuries before.

Like the Israelites, you may have been tolerating things for a long time. You may have repeatedly heard God's warning, but have never really come to the point of confession, repentance, and forgiveness. Now is the time to be radical. Now is the time to refuse the things you have tolerated. Now is the time to get straight with God.

CHAPTER 14

ENCOUNTER ON CARMEL

Mount Carmel is a fascinating place, a huge natural arena where people can gather in vast crowds and where a voice can carry easily. There is a well there, too. It contains water even when there is severe drought. No wonder Elijah chose to bring the nation together there for his extraordinary showdown with the priests of Baal.

"How long will you waver between two opinions? Let's decide the issue once and for all," Elijah challenged them. "The contest is between the Lord and Baal, and we'll worship and follow the winner—the one who answers with fire." So the priests of Baal danced, shouted, screamed, and slashed themselves, but there was no answer from Baal. Elijah mocked and laughed at them, and they shouted louder, but still there was no answer. Their agony lasted the whole day. Man-made gods never have answers. Generation after generation has created all kinds of deaf and hopeless gods who seem impressive until a real crisis comes along. Then they are futile.

Freedom—the Baal of today

"We want freedom!" That's the great cry today. People don't

want Christian morality. They hate the idea of constraint. They want to be free to "express themselves," to get drunk, take drugs, lie, cheat, sleep around. Modern man regards Christian ethics as repressive and harmful. "Freedom holds the answers," they claim. Man is coming of age and must be released from old-fashioned restraints.

If freedom is the answer, then the more of it we get, the better. But is this principle borne out in practice? Have the most "liberated" people discovered the answer? If you really want to know, pursue them. Try calling on their gods. Look at those who have gotten themselves into freedom in a big way.

Cry to alcohol, "Have you got the answers?" Then observe the experts—the people who have indulged themselves the most. Do they look as though they've found the answer? Look! There's one of them! He's sleeping on that park bench under some old newspapers. His breath stinks of booze. He's bound to know if drink is the answer.

Years ago that man was probably approached by a friend who said, "Let's go out and have some fun. You're free to enjoy yourself if you like. Let's go and get drunk." It was good fun at first, but as time passed, the drink began to take over. The poor man was thrown out of his home and separated from his family. Now he walks the streets by day and sleeps on a park bench at night. He wanted to be free, so he cried out to drink. He sang and shouted and staggered around. But drink provided no answer.

So what about drugs? Do they have the answer? Some say, "Drugs should be made legal. Let's experiment. Let's have a few kicks now and then. It doesn't do any harm. It really sets you free. Here, have a try. It's like paradise."

Is it? While I was at London Bible College a group of us used to spend Saturday nights evangelizing in a coffee bar in the West End. One evening I watched a young man inject himself. He told me that he knew he would die before he was twenty-five. He wanted to be free, so he cried out to dope. He danced in ecstasy and pierced his skin. But drugs offered him no answer.

Then there are people who want the freedom to gratify their

sexual desires. "Let's sleep around," they say. "And how about getting into intimate relationships with members of our own sex? It's about time people respected homosexuals and accepted their practices as normal."

So they experiment. A social worker told me that homosexuals change partners much more often than heterosexuals; that's why AIDS affects so many so fast. So it isn't long before these advocates of free sex become enslaved by their freedom. They wander around hospital wards, longing for someone to find a cure to the virus, waiting to die. They wanted to be free, so they cried out to sex. But now they weep and curse the day when they began to experiment, because sex offered them no answer.

"Let's get into mysticism," say some people. "Hey, this guru is really way out. He teaches you to let your mind roam free. Why don't you try it?" The Beatles tried it. Did they find the answer?

India is rich in minerals and other resources. She could be a mighty nation. But walk through the streets of Bombay and what do you find? Terrible poverty and suffering. You are crazy if you think that eastern religion will give you freedom. If what you see there is the solution, that's pitiful. Go ahead; cry out to the many idols if you want to. But they will offer you no answer.

Others are experimenting with spiritualism. "Look, the glass has spelled out my name," they say. "There must be something in it. I think it's about time I consulted that medium in town. Maybe she could read my palm or contact my dead relative. Wow! The occult is a fascinating subject. I really feel I could find some answers in it."

Why, then, do so many of these occult worshipers live in such fear and feel that their lives are dominated by evil forces? Why do they explain to the media, "I heard a voice within urging me to do that awful thing"? Why do they commit suicide? They cried out to spiritualism, but it offered them no answer.

Shout as much as you like. Whip yourself into a frenzy. Scream out for answers. You will not find any out there. Baal remains silent. And while he does, the prescriptions for drugs multiply at a phenomenal rate with many millions of people becoming dependent on them. That's the price society is paying for abandoning Christian values in favor of a fruitless worship of freedom.

Send the fire!

Elijah used twelve stones to rebuild the altar of the Lord that had been torn down. "Look," he was implying, "this is symbolic of the twelve tribes of Israel. I'm taking you back to your heritage, reminding you that you're the covenant people of God, calling you to return to him."

The people desperately wanted water, but Elijah knew that before water could come, they needed fire. Their sin had to be judged. God's wrath had to fall on an innocent sacrifice, so the prophet took a sacrificial animal, cut it in pieces, laid it on the altar, and poured water over it. Then he called to God to send the fire. This was not the only time in the Old Testament that fire fell from heaven. When the first priests were ordained, Aaron sacrificed to God, and "fire came out from the presence of the Lord and consumed the burnt offering and the fat portions on the altar" (Lev. 9:24).

When David sinned against the Lord by numbering the people, God judged them by sending a plague. David repented, built an altar, and sacrificed burnt offerings and fellowship offerings. "He called on the Lord, and the Lord answered him with fire from heaven on the altar of burnt offering" (1 Chron. 21:26).

Solomon stood before the altar of the Lord and dedicated the temple to him. When he had finished praying, "fire came down from heaven and consumed the burnt offering and the sacrifices, and the glory of the Lord filled the temple" (2 Chron. 7:1).

"At the time of sacrifice, the prophet Elijah stepped forward and prayed: 'O Lord, God of Abraham, Isaac and Israel, let it be known today that you are God in Israel and that I am your servant and have done all these things at your command. Answer me, O Lord, answer me, so these people will know that you, O Lord, are God, and that you are turning their hearts back again" (1 Kings 18:36,37).

At last there was an answer! God heard his servant and in his great mercy accepted the innocent sacrifice. He sent the fire. "I will receive this sacrifice," he said. "It pleases me. It will atone for your sin. Now, get rid of the evil prophets and pray for rain."

Send the rain!

When the Lord answered by fire, the Israelites knew that he was God and they slew the false prophets. What was Ahab's reaction to all this? Did he fall down and exclaim with the people, "The Lord—he is God! The Lord—he is God!" Probably not.

Elijah said to Ahab, "Go, eat and drink, for there is the sound of a heavy rain" (1 Kings 18:41). Elijah knew him. "Off you go," he said. "You'll be more interested in your dinner than in what has happened here today." Ahab should have been on his face, pleading for mercy, crying, "Oh, God. What have I done to this nation?" But there was no sign of remorse, no sign of repentance, no sign of any reaction at all.

Standing there on Mount Carmel, Ahab must have been a pathetic sight. The fire had fallen, the people had acknowledged the Lord, the false prophets had been slaughtered, and now the rain was on its way. There was the king of the nation, untouched, unmoved, unchanged. "Eat and drink," said Elijah. "All right," replied Ahab, and trotted off to do just that (1 Kings 18:42).

While Ahab went off to satisfy his stomach, Elijah went to pray. His job was not yet complete. He spoke a word of faith that rain was on its way, but now he would pray it into being, humbling himself before his God in fervent intercession.

What a contrast we have here. Two men attend the same event—the unequivocal demonstration of the futility of Baal; the prolonged and passionate pleading of the Baalite priests that went unanswered; the unmasking of the false god and his spiritually bankrupt followers. They both witness the extraordinary miracle of fire actually falling from heaven, burning up not only the water-sodden sacrifice but the very wood and stones as well. Yet their responses are completely opposite. You may wonder how a man can be so indifferent to the workings of God.

The very cross of Christ stood between the scoffer on one side and the penitent thief on the other. Both witness the world-changing sufferings of the Lamb of God. One is humbled, the other hardened. But it will always be so until Jesus comes and separates the sheep from the goats forever.

The warning is trumpeted loud and clear: Keep a humble heart lest you should ever find yourself witnessing the activity of God but failing to recognize it when it is right before you. Let us worship God acceptably, with reverence and awe, for he is a consuming fire (Heb. 12:28,29).

CHAPTER 15

REACHING ROCK BOTTOM

One moment our great hero is standing confidently on Mount Carmel calling down fire from heaven; the next he is a terrified man running for his life towards the desert.

Yes. "Elijah was a man just like us" (James 5:17). On Mount Carmel he looked like someone out of this world. But now we recognize flesh and blood, and suddenly we can identify with him.

So where did Elijah go wrong? Here was a man whom God had trained to bear up under pressure. "Give me your son," he had said to the widow during his training period. "Come here to me," he had said to the nation on Mount Carmel. Elijah invited pressure, so why did he suddenly collapse under it? One thing is sure: like Peter on the lake, his eyes must have drifted away from the Lord. But why?

Did he become angry?

God's judgment may sometimes seem harsh, but it is always flawless and is always motivated by love. As imperfect human beings, we frequently find it hard to express righteous anger. Someone sins and we confront him, but we allow our own feelings of hostility to take over. So instead of loving the sinner and hating the sin, we lash out and condemn both.

Did Elijah fall into this trap? When he challenged the priests of Baal, did he slip from God's holy wrath into his own anger and frustration?

When taking your stand against modern evils, beware of adopting a judgmental spirit and working off your own personal frustrations and pet hatreds. Never forget that God hates sin but still loves sinners. How often have overly zealous "evangelists" given people the impression that a vindictive God is totally against them?

Did he become proud?

Elijah had spent three years concealed from the public eye. All his previous miracles were worked in private—by a hidden stream, or in a widow's humble home.

Suddenly, Elijah faced not seclusion but overwhelming public triumph and vindication. An obscure prophet suddenly became the most famous man in the land.

Perhaps you have been hidden away for a while. Maybe your whole church used to meet in a living room, but now it's the biggest in town. Maybe you have begun to be used with words of knowledge or prayers for the sick. Now others are beginning to seek you out; you are getting a reputation. How are you handling it? Once you begin to gain popularity it can easily go to your head.

Elijah's early ministry was characterized by God-consciousness. But at some point, did he suddenly become self-conscious? As he shot past the kings's chariot did he think, "Hey, Ahab. Look at me. I'm motoring!" Elijah hadn't had a public ministry before. But now the spotlight was on him. Beware the secret ambition for recognition.

Did he become exhausted?

Elijah may simply have been worn out. For three years he had been living under the pressure of a drought that he had announced. Then came the emotional buildup to Carmel, as the news traveled slowly across the nation without the aid of radio or television. This was followed by the emotional demands of the day itself. Finally there was the crushing realization that Ahab and Jezebel were untouched and unchanged. Elijah was emotionally shattered.

Disappointments

Elijah probably set all his hopes on the confrontation between God and the priests of Baal. "This will turn the nation," he thought. "Everyone will worship the Lord now." Then, when Ahab and Jezebel showed no signs of repentance, the tremendous miracle seemed to come to be for nothing, and Elijah collapsed.

Disappointment drains you. Let's say you decide on a special gospel outreach. Someone slaves over a dramatic script; others prepare music and slide sequences. People are praying and rehearsing hard, giving all their energies in order to make the event successful. Leaflets are printed and delivered around the neighborhood. Hostesses and coffee-makers are appointed, and someone even gives up three hours of her time to buy and arrange some flowers in the hall. By the evening everything is ready. Expectations run high. The doors are flung wide—and a handful of people stroll in.

The following Sunday the church meets as usual. "Terrific evenings, weren't they?" says everyone. "The performances were superb." But inside you are thinking, "The performances were great, but where were the audiences? We worked so hard—the babysitting, the costumes, the rehearsals. Was it all for nothing?" And if the truth be known, you are drained and deeply disappointed.

We can even be disappointed by our nearest and dearest. Lack of appreciation in marriage is very hard to bear. "She doesn't appreciate me," says the husband. "I'm out all day, coping with the pressure, making important decisions, battling to keep on top of the work. I come home exhausted, wanting some time to

unwind. I pick up the paper, and all she can talk about is her day."
"He doesn't appreciate me," says his wife. "I'm stuck here all day, coping with the kids, changing diapers, doing the washing, ironing, cleaning, shopping, cooking. . . . No, don't touch that, Peter! Yes, it is pretty, Susan. James, leave that alone! It'll fall over. Yes it will. It has! Now stop crying. It's only hurting a little bit. Let's kiss and make it better. . . . And after a day of this my husband comes in, flops on the sofa, picks up the paper, and asks, 'Is dinner ready?' He doesn't care about me. He doesn't understand what I go through all day long. All he wants is my body. He doesn't appreciate me at all." Disappointment leads to bitterness and hostility. Spiritual collapse is about to take place.

Delays and dilemmas
"Hope deferred makes the heart sick," (Prov. 13:12) as anyone knows who has waited endlessly for their house to sell or for another job to turn up.

Often you can see why things happen to you. It's raining hard. The bus shoots past the end of your road and you charge after it in hot pursuit. It stops, takes two passengers on board, and pulls away just before you arrive. You stop dead, panting, sopping wet. The rain slithers down your neck and your face reflects a mixture of pain and despair. You stand wearily under the bus shelter. A woman joins you.

Woman: I suppose we've missed the bus.
You: Yes.
Woman: You live around here, don't you?
You: That's right. Just around the corner.
Woman: I thought so. I'm sure I've seen you go past my house to that church.
You: Yes. I'm a member there.
Woman: Oh, are you? They always seem such a happy crowd. Tell me more about it.

And suddenly you know why you missed the bus. "Oh, it's a divine appointment," you say to yourself. "I'd miss any number of buses for a divine appointment. Now where are my tracts?"

When you know the reason for what happened, you are happy. The problem arises when you stand at the bus stop for forty-five minutes and no one else turns up. Or you go to the hospital and you think, "I really want to witness to the patients here," but you are so ill that it's as much as you can do to ask for a glass of water. "What's the point?" you think. Perplexity saps you of your strength.

Living at today's pace

Every generation encounters the pressures of life, but no generation has had to cope with stress as much as has ours. Wherever you go you find people struggling to stay on top, packing as much as they can into every available minute. Fred Mitchell, the former leader of the Overseas Missionary Fellowship, had a plaque in his office. It read, "Beware the barrenness of a busy life."

By contemporary standards, the pace of life in Jesus' time on earth was relatively steady. If he wanted to go from one place to another, he would have to walk, ride, or sail. Today one new invention replaces another, and the pace of life races forward ever faster. My father remembered the first car to come through our home town. He was also alive when the Concorde broke the sound barrier and when men walked on the moon.

Christians are trying to glorify God in the midst of this hectic experience. It has proved too demanding for many who, like Elijah, have suffered total collapse of the inner self. The computer generation has a severe headache. God views all this with tenderness and compassion.

Wilderness

Something made Elijah take his eyes off the Lord, and he fled into the wilderness, a despondent and frightened man. As he ran, his young servant's questioning eyes probed his soul. "What are you doing, Elijah? Mount Carmel was great. The fire fell, and now the rain has come—wonderful! But where are we going now?" I can hear Elijah saying, "Stop looking at me like that. I can't stand it. You stay here." Elijah went on alone. Sometimes when you are running away there are eyes you would rather not look into.

Leaving his servant behind, Elijah ran into a physical and spiritual desert. "He came to a broom tree, sat down under it and prayed that he might die. 'I have had enough, Lord,' he said. 'Take my life; I am no better than my ancestors'" (1 Kings 19:4). Having lost all sense of purpose, he felt condemned and worthless. It was then, when he was most vulnerable, that the devil moved in maliciously and brought him to the brink of suicide.

"I might as well be dead." I wonder how many of us have ever gotten that far. A single parent, at the end of her rope and on the point of ending her life, holds on only because, "What would happen to the children if I killed myself?" But she has long since given up on herself. A man, unemployed for many months, reaches the stage where he wonders, "My life is totally purposeless. Why not end it all?" A young couple, in deep debt and relentlessly pursued by the financiers, question, "Why are we here? We can't overcome this problem. There's no future. We might as well be dead."

The devil comes to steal, kill, and destroy (John 10:10). He appears on the scene when we are our weakest because at that time he has the greatest chance of success.

Elijah had reached rock bottom. But God did not answer his suicide prayer, nor did he condemn him for his negative attitude. Instead, he treated Elijah with great understanding, tenderness, and compassion. He also fully restored him to peace, joy, and purpose; but more of that in our next chapter.

CHAPTER 16

YOUR GENTLENESS MADE ME GREAT

When David was chasing the Amalekites, he and his followers came across an exhausted man in a field. They gave him food and water and then asked him why he was there. He replied, "I am an Egyptian, the slave of an Amalekite. My master abandoned me when I became ill three days ago" (1 Sam. 30:13).

Elijah's Master could so easily have done the same. If God were like us, Elijah would probably have been fired, but that is not his style. When Elijah ran out of gas, he ran straight into grace! And grace never gives up, never ignores, never backs off. Whenever wounded people run into grace, they run into the arms of God, who knows exactly what to do.

Refreshment

Before giving him spiritual instruction, God remembered that Elijah needed rest, food, and time, so he gave him all three before saying a thing.

The God of the Bible "makes me lie down in green pastures...he restores my soul" (Ps. 23:2,3) and "grants sleep to those he loves" (Ps. 127:2). So often we can be tempted to think that relating to

115

God is all spiritual gymnastics—a frenzy of praying, fasting, and witnessing. But that's not true. We must get to know the God who lets us lie down and gives us sleep.

Having slept soundly, Elijah awoke to the touch of an angel who had prepared a meal for him. Having given the prophet rest, God now provided nourishment. The Lord knows our body's needs. He created those needs and he fulfills them. Beware the super-spirituality that looks exclusively for the supernatural answer and ignores the human side, including a good rest and nourishing food.

What is more, the meal was prepared by an angel. When Elijah was at the center of God's will at the Kerith Ravine, he was fed with bits of food by ravens. When he ran for his life, disobedient and dejected, God did not dispatch another raven but commissioned an angel. That's grace.

The devil tells us that when we fail God, we have to suffer for it. "You've really done it this time," he tells us. "You can't expect any more provision from God. Face it; you're on your own. What a shame. You were showing such potential."

What lies! When we fail, Jesus does not keep us at arm's length; instead, he comes to us. Look at Peter. He cursed and swore that he didn't know Jesus. Did Jesus reject him? No. After the Resurrection, Jesus stood on the seashore and called to the disciples in the boat, "Come and have breakfast" (John 21:12). He did not say, "Peter, you disowned me, so you can't join us."

The good shepherd was lovingly regathering his flock. The disciples had been in a boat all night. They needed food, and Jesus was there to give it to them. Elijah, too, had been working hard. He also needed refreshment, and God was there to give it to him.

Once Elijah had slept and eaten, God did not immediately close in on him. He let him run. He gave the prophet space—forty days and nights—to get the whole thing out of his system. "Come on, Elijah," he said. "Just run. Work out the tension. You'll feel better for it." And Elijah ran. Counselors, take note of some of God's ways of restoring a man.

Foundation

Now that he had been refreshed by God, Elijah was no longer running aimlessly into the wilderness. He ran back to his roots: to Horeb, where God first spoke to Moses from the burning bush and made a covenant with the Israelites, giving them the Ten Commandments (Deut. 5:2-4). Elijah was going back to his foundation.

When you are perplexed and disillusioned you must run to things you know are true. You cannot stay in the wilderness. Remember the foundations of your faith. Remind yourself, "Hey! I've been born again! Didn't Jesus say to his followers, 'I am with you always'? Isn't he the same yesterday, today, and forever? So what am I doing allowing life to toss me around? Why am I carrying on as though I'm standing on shifting sand? There's a solid Rock over there. I've got to get back to it, back to God, because with him there's a foundation stone on which I know I can stand. I don't know why the job fell through. . . don't know why he's developed cancer. . . don't know why the engagement failed. . . But I do know that God is my fortress." Or, as Job responded, even in his suffering, "I know that my redeemer lives."

You are not following an abstract philosophy. You are in a covenant relationship with a God who acts in history, a person to whom you can run. Many Christians waste weeks, months, even years through neglect of this truth. "I have a covenant-keeping God. He will not fail me." Upon such bedrock you can stand.

Identity and accountability

Now Elijah was ready to hear from God. He was rested and nourished, and had run back to the roots of his faith. God met him with a question: "What are you doing here, Elijah?"

Elijah had come to the place where he said of himself, "I'm nothing. I'm hopeless. I'm an emotional mess. I might as well be dead." But God said of him, "No. You are Elijah. You are not a nothing. You are a person and you have a name and a history.

Not only that, you are my servant. You are accountable to me, so what are you doing here?" God knew that Elijah's thoughts about himself were not true. He had run away, yes, but he was not a hopeless mess. He was God's servant, and God wanted him to see anew the dignity of his identity.

God wants you to know that you are not, as many modern philosophers suggest, simply a lot of feelings and thoughts happening one after the other. A mass of feelings has no identity, but you do, and with identity comes accountability. One day you will stand before God and give account of what you did with your life, how you used the talents God gave you. The awareness of that truth should stir you out of the complacency and lethargy that can swamp your soul after a period of discouragement.

"The fear of the Lord teaches a man wisdom" (Prov. 15:33). We dare not become so bound by self-pity that we lose our holy fear of God and stop serving him. For some, this medicine may be hard to take, but it will bring ultimate healing. God first gave Elijah rest, food, and space, and then asked him, "What are you doing here?" He made him face up to reality.

Intimacy

Following an awesome display of power which tore the mountains apart and shattered the rocks, God drew Elijah near with a gentle whisper. It was not the magnificent display of power that drew Elijah to the mouth of the cave, but the soft voice that spoke to him of God's tenderness and love, reminding us of King David's testimony, "Your gentleness has made me great" (Ps. 18:35, NKJV).

Accountability to God must be accompanied by intimacy with him, because we will receive healing and restoration only when the two are brought together. We must hear the voice that asks, "What are you doing here? Don't you realize that you are answerable to me for your conduct?" But we must also have our ears tuned to the gentle whisper that says, "You are precious to me. I know what's happening"—and that woos us tenderly back into God's purposes.

God is not interested merely in how you can serve him. He wants you to hear the clear, gentle whisper, "I love you. I'm for you. I know your sighing, your longings, your heartbreak. I know what you've been doing for me and how little you've been appreciated for it. I hear you when you cry out in desperation." It's this gentle whisper that melts your heart.

David said, "He rescued me because he delighted in me" (Ps. 18:19). That is one of the greatest truths in the whole Bible: God is delighted with you. When God whispers into your ear, "I'm delighted with you," it's almost too much to bear. He adds, "You will be called by a new name: my delight is in you'" (See Isa. 62:2,4).

I once looked up "delight" in the dictionary. It said, "great pleasure and satisfaction." But I wasn't too pleased or satisfied with that. So I searched for it in a thesaurus. This is what I found: "laugh, smile, get a kick out of, hug oneself, rave, bask in, enjoy, wallow, have fun, exhilarate, relish, elate, thrill, ravish, intoxicate, entrance, enrapture, purr." Isn't that wonderful? When God looks at us, he purrs with delight!

Have you ever fallen in love? You are in a room full of people and suddenly you realize, "She saw me!" The Bible says, "You have stolen my heart, my sister, my bride; you have stolen my heart with one glance of your eyes" (Song of Songs 4:9). Or have you ever seen parents with their first baby? "Isn't he wonderful? Doesn't he look like me? Did you see that? That was his first smile." God purrs over us like that.

How do I find healing from exhaustion? It's in the gentle whisper from God, "I love you. I'm delighted with you. You make my heart sing whenever I see you." That's what has overwhelmed great Christians in history. And that's what restores your soul— a fresh experience of intimacy with God and a new revelation of his love.

Commission

God drew Elijah close to him; then, to complete the prophet's restoration, he gave him a job to do. He did the same for Peter, who must have thought, "After what I've done, Jesus will never trust or use me again." But Jesus, having reestablished a loving relationship with his disciple, said to him, "Feed my sheep" (John 21:17). Peter must have been stunned to hear those words, repeated three times so that he really got the message: "I still want to use you." Little did he know just how greatly he would be used. He would never have dreamed that he—the one who denied Jesus before a handful of people—would within a few weeks be preaching to a vast crowd in central Jerusalem and seeing three thousand converted.

"Go back the way you came," God told Elijah (1 Kings 19:15). Then he continued, "When you get there . . . ." This was no vague commission, a sort of pat on the head and a general comment, "Off you go. You'll find your way somehow." No, there was a specific job for Elijah to do. I expect that in his desolation he thought, "I'm finished. I will certainly never speak to a king again." In fact, Elijah's new commission did not consist merely of addressing one king but of anointing two. (1 Kings 19:15,16). Furthermore, while he had come to regard his life as worthless, God regarded it as worth reproducing. He was going to give him a disciple—Elisha. Some commentators say that the two prophets spent ten years working together. One failure had not destroyed all the excellent characteristics that God had built into Elijah, nor have any feelings of desolation you have recently experienced nullified all that God has taught you over the years.

"Furthermore," God was telling his servant, "you have been on your own long enough, so I'm giving you a friend, someone you can care for and train to take over from you. Contrary to your expectations, your ministry has not finished. I want you to stop thinking about yourself and start concentrating on Elisha. He doesn't know as much about me as you do. I want you to give yourself to him, praying for him and teaching him everything you know. And by the way, you're not as alone in the work as you make out. There are still seven thousand people in Israel who refuse to worship Baal."

Restoration

God has a wonderful way of working healing into weary people. If you drift away from him, he does not abandon you. No matter what you do, you are always his delightful child—but do not take advantage of that fact, because one day you will give account of yourself to him.

"Lazarus, come out!" Jesus commanded (John 11:43). He did not say, "Corpse, come out!" Lazarus had a name, an identity, and so do we. From inside our tomb, we may protest, "But I can't come out. I stink. Look at me. I might as well be dead." But God will have none of it. "Come out!" he says to us. "Come out of that despondency, that self-pity, that sense of uselessness. Tombs are not meant for people who are alive in Christ and who still have work to do for me. Leave the tomb behind and come back into the light. My thoughts about you have never changed. I still love you. I'm still delighted with you. I still want to use you to establish my kingdom. So, come out!"

CHAPTER 17

GO AND MAKE DISCIPLES

Relay racing must be among the most exciting of all the competitive sports. I love watching the runners hurtling around the track, slapping the baton into the hand of the next man, panting with exhaustion but straining to see if their team will finally win.

The technique of baton-passing is very crucial. Within brief seconds safe communication must take place from the one who has finished his course to the one who is just beginning. For fleeting moments they run together, then the fresh athlete is away. Races are often won or lost in those vital exchanges. Pure speed around the track can never win such a race. In this team event, you must make sure you have grasped what was passed on to you.

Pass the baton

God's plans go beyond the part played by individuals. Naturally, you want to fulfill God's purpose for your life, but do not think that he is concerned only about your leg of the race. Passing on the baton is part of your job. It cannot be allowed to fall. It must be passed, received, and carried on.

From early times, God wove this principle firmly into the lives of his people. Fathers were given very clear instructions on how to raise their families: "Impress [these commandments] on your children. Talk about them when you sit at home and when you walk along the road, when you lie down and when you get up" (Deut. 6:7). So the fathers were to tell their children, "We are God's special people, his light to the nations, and he has given us his holy laws to follow. This is the lifestyle he wants us to have. These are his commandments. I'm teaching you these things so that you will obey them and in turn teach them to your children after you" (See Deut. 4:9). As children quickly grow up and leave the family home, you realize how rapidly the baton-passing opportunity is gone. Don't miss it.

Not only were fathers exhorted to pass on God's commandments, they were also to recount his mighty acts. "We will tell the next generation. . . the wonders he has done" (Ps. 78:4). They were to tell succeeding generations about the escape from Egypt, the parting of the Red Sea, the crossing of the Jordan, the taking of Jericho. They also had to pass on the great hope of Israel, the glorious future awaiting them when the Messiah came.

Children were similarly instructed to take note of what they were told. "Honor your father and your mother," God commanded them (Ex. 20:12). In other words, "When they teach you about me, don't turn your back on them. Honor them and take their words seriously." Scripture also advises, "A wise son heeds his father's instruction," and, "He who ignores discipline despises himself" (Prov. 13:1, 15:32).

Certainly Moses made sure that the Israelites understood the law of God, but he had more than that to pass on. Resting upon this national leader was a gift, an anointing from the Holy Spirit, and God wanted that anointing to rest on Moses' successor. When Moses knew that Joshua would be the next leader of the nation, he laid hands on him, and Joshua was "filled with the spirit of wisdom" (Deut. 34:9).

God wants to raise up leaders, but sadly, leaders are sometimes hard to find. The book of Judges records a dark period in Israel's history. Leaders occasionally emerged, but none of them imparted anything of any real value to the next generation. Gideon came and went; so too did Samson. For a while the nation profited from their leadership, but then it fell away because no one was building on the foundation that the previous man had laid. The final comment in the book is a sad reflection on the state of a directionless people: "In those days Israel had no king; everyone did as he saw fit" (Judg. 21:25). When leaders simply dropped the baton and died, the nation lost its way again. All that these men had learned about God died with them. How many mighty men of God through the ages have taken most of their secrets with them to the grave instead of passing them on like valued family treasures?

At this point in Elijah's story, God had already chosen his successor, the man who would carry on his prophetic ministry, and Elijah spent maybe ten years with him. The next phase of God's plan for the nation had to continue through a new servant, Elisha, and part of Elijah's calling was to make him an excellent disciple.

Make disciples

In recent years, "discipleship" has spelled trouble. If you even mention it in some churches, you are likely to encounter a mass retreat; many cautionary stories have circulated concerning people whose lives have been ruined by so-called discipleship.

Through fear of excessive domination of people's lives, many have steered clear of discipleship, but how can we back off from a subject that is so clearly biblical? "Disciple" is used over 250 times in the New Testament. On ten occasions John the Baptist's disciples are mentioned, on four occasions Paul's, while the rest are disciples of Jesus. The Twelve were not told, "Go and preach sermons and give out literature." They were commissioned to "go and make disciples" (Matt. 28:19). Jesus didn't want his followers merely to pass on information; he wanted them involved in the formation of lives. So Paul instructed Timothy, "The things you have heard me say. . . entrust to reliable men who will also be qualified to teach others" (2 Tim. 2:2).

Discipleship has generated controversy in some circles due to fear of the abuse of authority, yet we dare not react, "Oh, discipleship is a dangerous subject. We'll just give these new Christians a Bible to read, pray for them, and trust God to keep them straight." A new believer doesn't want someone to give him a Bible and desert him because "discipleship is a risky business." He desperately needs help, and we must obey the original instruction to make disciples. The command came from Jesus himself, so we have no choice.

The story of Elijah and Elisha gives us an excellent model of discipling.

Who initiates?

Elijah never thought to himself, "I've had enough of being a prophet. It's too exhausting. I'm going to find someone else to take over from me." Nor did Elisha charge up to Elijah and urge him, "Please let me be your disciple. Let me have the cloak. Please!" No. The initiator was God, and he spoke first to Elijah.

God worked in the same way with Moses and Joshua. Moses did not choose Joshua, but neither did Joshua force himself on Moses. It began with God, who spoke first to Moses. Then Moses, in turn, spoke to Joshua.

Early on in his ministry, Jesus was pursued by the multitudes. Then, one evening he went out and prayed all night on a mountainside. "When morning came, he called his disciples to him and chose twelve of them, whom he designated apostles" (Luke 6:13). It's likely that there were many more than twelve people who wanted to be Jesus' disciples, but he made his own selection.

Timothy did not approach Paul, saying, "Can I work alongside you, please?" Rather, Paul took the initiative and taught Timothy to do the same (2 Tim. 2:1,2).

To be consistent with Scripture, you must not wait for would-be disciples to come to you with the request, "Please disciple me." Indeed, you are not obliged to respond to anyone who is seeking this sort of relationship. You can, of course, remain good friends and coworkers with them, but the Bible clearly shows a pattern we would do well to follow.

If you respond to a request from anyone for discipleship training, you may not find faith that it's going to work. You cannot say, "God started this," and therefore be assured of success. But when God indicates his choice, you can proceed with faith because you have responded to God's initiative. Since the undertaking is rooted in God's will, faith and expectation for the disciple's development will naturally run high.

If you accept anyone who comes to you for discipleship training, you could find yourself at the mercy of other people's expectations and demands and become vulnerable and accountable to them. Thus a relationship intended to be a joy and a privilege could in reality become an exhausting and burdensome round of activity not rooted in faith.

Working with God

When you know that God has initiated a relationship, you can also expect his help. You do not have to make the disciple over-dependent on you. You become a fellow laborer with God in producing another disciple of the Lord Jesus.

"Who do people say the Son of man is?" Jesus asked his disciples (Matt. 16:13). Peter replied, "You are the Christ, the Son of the living God" (Matt. 16:16). On hearing this, Jesus said to Peter, "Blessed are you, Simon son of Jonah, for this was not revealed to you by man, but by my Father in heaven" (Matt. 16:17). Jesus was the discipler, but Peter found out something that Jesus had never told him. He received a revelation from God. Similarly, when your disciple finds out things you did not tell him, don't become offended but rejoice that God is working alongside you. Ultimately your goal is to help the new believer hear and obey God for himself. You want to present him as one who has become mature, no longer dependent on you.

God wants discipleship training to be an integral part of the life of every healthy church. Just as Jesus hand-picked and trained the men he wanted for discipling others, so disciplers should be trained and commissioned by the church before they are released to train others.

Not everyone should be encouraged to disciple others. The apostle Paul warned the Ephesian elders, "After I leave, savage wolves will come in among you and will not spare the flock. Even from your own number men will arise and distort the truth in order to draw away disciples after them" (Acts 20:29,30). Beware of lone disciplers who seek a personal following.

What's the goal?

God told Elijah that Elisha would succeed him as prophet (1 Kings 19:16). To Elijah, this was not just a nice idea. It was his commission. Right from the word go, he knew exactly what he had to produce, and that goal would set the pattern for the training. After three years, Elijah could review his disciple's progress and ask himself, "Is Elisha more like a prophet now than when I found him?"

Discipleship must have an objective. If a discipler doesn't know what he's trying to produce, how can he test his disciple's progress? Your goal is not to place someone in permanent subordination but to prepare him for usefulness.

Elijah knew exactly what he was trying to make: a prophet to take his place. That knowledge gave both him and Elisha a firm foundation for the time they spent together. God told Moses, "Commission Joshua, and encourage and strengthen him, for he will lead this people across and will cause them to inherit the land" (Deut. 3:28).

"I charge you," said David to Solomon (1 Chron. 28:8). He then gave his son the plans for the work on the temple, and continued, "Be strong and courageous, and do the work" (1 Chron. 28:20). David left Solomon with no doubts about what he was meant to accomplish. Then he encouraged him to do it.

Paul said to Timothy, "I give you this charge: Preach the word; be prepared in season and out of season; correct, rebuke and encourage—with great patience and careful instruction. . . discharge all the duties of your ministry" (2 Tim. 4:1,2,5). Timothy knew what he was meant to be doing before he received the encouragement, "The Lord be with your spirit. Grace be with you" (2 Tim. 4:22).

When Jesus sent out the Twelve, he first gave them specific instructions about what they should and should not do. "Do not go to the Gentiles or to the Samaritans but to the Israelites," he said. "Tell them that the kingdom of heaven is near. Heal people, raise the dead, and drive out demons. Take this, don't take that. Beware of men. Keep going. . ." (Matt. 10:1-28).

Then, having given them a definite goal, he continued, "Are not two sparrows sold for a penny? Yet not one of them will fall to the ground apart from the will of your Father. And even the very hairs of your head are all numbered. So don't be afraid; you are worth more than many sparrows" (Matt. 10:29-31). First Jesus commissioned his disciples, then he offered words to encourage them.

Close companionship

God did not say to Elisha, "I think I'll send you to one of the schools of the prophets. Which would you prefer—Bethel, Jericho, or Jordan?" Clearly these groups did exist (2 Kings 2:3,5,7) and accurately prophesied that Elijah would be taken up into heaven. But God wanted Elisha to learn from personal involvement with his anointed servant. He was going to take Elijah's cloak, Elijah's place. He was not going to receive information alone; he was going to acquire something of Elijah's spirit.

Paul wrote to the Corinthians, "I am sending to you Timothy, my son whom I love, who is faithful in the Lord. He will remind you of my way of life in Christ Jesus, which agrees with what I teach everywhere in every church. . . . He is carrying on the work of the Lord, just as I am. No one, then, should refuse to accept him" (1 Cor. 4:17; 16:10,11). Why should the church receive Timothy so readily? Because Paul's cloak rested on him. This young man had worked alongside the great apostle. He knew Paul's ways and would faithfully represent him.

Not possessive or exclusive

Although Elijah knew that Elisha was going to replace him in ministry, he was not possessive. "All right, Elisha, you've got to cling to me now. Keep away from that school of the prophets. Don't you dare listen to anybody except me. This is the way I do it. You just follow suit." It was not like that at all. When Elijah called Elisha, he threw his cloak over him, but he put no pressure on Elisha to go with him. He wanted Elisha to know from the start that discipleship would not bring him into frightening personal bondage, so he gave Elisha space, the chance to think about it, the freedom to turn back (1 Kings 19:20). He retained the same attitude to the end. On the very day of his triumphant ascension into the heavens, he made no demands on his young disciple. If anything, he tried to dissuade him from an overdeveloped personal commitment. But Elisha would not be sidetracked. He had come to love his master and freely followed him—but more of that in our next chapter.

This light touch on the reins continued throughout their relationship. Just before Elijah returned to heaven, he said to Elisha, "Stay here, the Lord has sent me to Bethel" (2 Kings 2:2). In other words, "You don't have to continue with me. I'm not forcing you." But Elisha would not leave his master. The disciple's devotion was tested twice more, when Elijah went to Jericho and the Jordan, but still Elisha refused to be left behind (2 Kings 2:4,6).

Discipleship is not about servanthood but about friendship. "I no longer call you servants," said the Great Discipler. "Instead I have called you friends" (John 15:15). Elijah wanted a relationship with Elisha that was based not on obligation but on love and trust. He therefore had to ensure that his disciple always had room to breathe, to hear from God himself. Since Elijah was training this young man to be a prophet, he could not constantly tell him what to say and do. Elisha would then have become totally dependent on his master for the voice of God, and the prophetic word would have died when Elijah died. But Elisha had to develop his own gifting, his own personal relationship with God. Only then would God's great purpose for him be realized.

CHAPTER 18

THE BONDS
OF RELATIONSHIP

God must have been delighted by the relationship that developed between Elijah and Elisha. But then, he knew what he was doing when he first put them together.

A willing heart

When Elijah first met him, Elisha was not sitting in a quiet meadow making daisy chains and dreaming about becoming famous. He was pushing a plow, taking responsibility, working hard, serving his father.

When Samuel summoned David, the young man was out tending his father's sheep. Maybe he knew that the rest of his brothers were with the great prophet. Maybe he wanted to be there, too. Whatever the case, David did not allow his desires to interfere with his everyday work. He had not been invited to the meeting with Samuel, but he didn't sit in his room and mope about it. He got on with the job that he had been given.

Some of the Thessalonian Christians did not follow suit. They became so preoccupied with Jesus' second coming that they almost gave up on the idea of working for a living. Paul rebuked them. "Such people we command and urge in the Lord Jesus Christ to settle down and earn the bread they eat" (2 Thess. 3:12). God uses responsible people. He notes the men and women who are reliable, who take their everyday work seriously and who prove it by their actions.

When Elijah's cloak fell over his shoulders, Elisha was quick to honor his parents. Realizing what was happening, he continued to show concern for them. "Let me kiss my father and mother goodbye," he said, "and then I will come with you" (1 Kings 19:20).

Although he took time to bid farewell to his parents, this by no means represented what Jesus would later describe as "putting one hand on the plow and looking back," thereby proving oneself unworthy of the kingdom (Luke 9:62). Elisha responded wholeheartedly. "That's it," he said to his family. "I've heard the call of God, and I've got to leave you. From now on my chief occupation is to be Elijah's disciple." Then he slaughtered his yoke of oxen, built a bonfire with the plowing equipment, cooked the meat on it, and gave it to the people.

True disciples of Christ must be 100 percent committed and must demonstrate their commitment by burning their bridges, giving Christ priority over everything else in their lives.

A serving spirit

Elisha didn't begin his discipleship by saying, "Okay, I've brought my notebook. Are we starting with Leviticus or Deuteronomy?" No. Up to this point he had been serving his father, and now he was happy to become Elijah's servant (1 Kings 19:21). It was later recorded of him, "He used to pour water on the hands of Elijah" (2 Kings 3:11). I did not fully understand that phrase until I washed my hands in a place in India where there were no taps. With lather all over my hands I wondered, "Now what do I do?" Then someone came and poured water over them for me. So Elisha just did the little, practical things for Elijah.

There is no record that Elisha put pressure on Elijah or pestered him with, "Hey, Elijah, when do we get to calling down fire from heaven?"

Just before Elijah was taken up to heaven, the prophets said to Elisha, "Do you know that the Lord is going to take your master from you today?" (2 Kings 2:3,5). Even after years, it was apparent to everyone that Elijah was still master and Elisha his servant. And Elisha accepted that. He didn't argue with what they had said, neither did he elevate himself as successor. Instead, he simply replied, "Yes, I know, but do not speak of it" (2 Kings 2:3,5).

Heartfelt affection

Three times Elijah gave Elisha the opportunity to leave him. "Stay here. I'm going on," he said. But Elisha would not leave him. It's hard to leave someone you love. "My father! My father!" Elisha cried as Elijah was taken away from him (2 Kings 2:12). By that time, he was so close to his master that he felt as though he were losing his own father.

When Paul wrote to Timothy he said, ". . . Night and day I constantly remember you in my prayers. Recalling your tears, I long to see you, so that I may be filled with joy" (2 Tim. 1:3,4). Paul was not ashamed to express his feelings. "You've become dear to me," he said. "I remember how you cried when we parted for a while. I just want you to know that I love you and long to see you."

On another occasion, when Paul was about to leave the elders at Ephesus, he told them that they would never see him again. What was their reaction? "Oh. . . er. . . well, who's preaching next Sunday, then?" No! "They all wept as they embraced him and kissed him" (Acts 20:37). They shared their emotions. They expressed their love.

"My father! My father!" Elisha cried, as if to say, "What am I going to do without you? It's so painful to think that you're not going to be here any more."

Many people find it hard to express their feelings or to show their emotions. Embarrassed to weep in public, we refuse to say words that reflect what's really going on in our hearts. Indeed, many of us really don't allow people to get close to us, and so rob ourselves of the profound riches of heartfelt Christian fellowship and expressed love.

Was Elijah's heart always tender and loving? Maybe not. When we first met him, he seemed to be a lonely, rock-like individual. It's possible that God had to work on him, to soften him and give him a deep affection for Elisha. God can change stones into sons (Matt. 3:9). He can take hard, defensive hearts and make them tender, loving, and outgoing.

An honoring relationship

Intimate friendship and warm affection between people can sometimes dull the edge of the respect that should also be shown. A delicate balance is required lest familiarity breed contempt and in our modern informality we fail to genuinely honor God's chosen servants. Intimacy should never destroy esteem. Elisha did not talk flippantly about his master. He did not sigh, "At last, God is taking him! It will be so good to get rid of the old boy. He was getting a bit staid in his ways, and it's about time I moved into my ministry."

As Elijah was taken up, his cloak fell to the ground. Elisha picked it up but didn't say, "Oh, this is the old cloak he used to wear. It's so dated. Surely it's about time we got into some modern gear, some new ways. This old thing can go." No, Elisha honored his master even in this. He respected Elijah's greater experience of life, picked up what he had left behind, and carried it through into his own ministry.

When Elijah asked Elisha, "What can I do for you before I am taken from you?" Elisha replied, "Let me inherit a double portion of your spirit" (2 Kings 2:9,10). Elisha surely had seen Elijah on his off days, when no one would have wanted his spirit. Yet he still honored his master and wanted to share the blessing he saw in Elijah's life.

As Elijah was taken up into heaven, Elisha cried out, "My father! My father! The chariots and horsemen of Israel!" (2 Kings 2:12). He was not referring to the chariot he saw, but to Elijah himself.

He was saying, "We don't trust in chariots and horses but in the living God. Elijah, you are God's prophet, God's mouthpiece; therefore you are the defense of Israel. My father, I love you. I honor your great ministry."

A fruitful relationship

When Elijah had gone, Elisha took on his role as Israel's defense. In his lifetime great armies came against the nation, but they could not penetrate it because Elisha warned what was going to happen before it occurred. The king of Aram couldn't understand how the Israelites could possibly know all about his secret invasion plans until he was told, "Elisha, the prophet who is in Israel, tells the king of Israel the very words you speak in your bedroom" (2 Kings 6:12). When Elisha became ill, "the king of Israel went down to see him and wept over him. 'My father! My father!' he cried. 'The chariots and horsemen of Israel!' (2 Kings 13:14)." In other words, "You are our defense. We honor you as God's prophet. We respect you and your ministry."

The discipleship worked! God told Elijah that Elisha would succeed him as prophet, and he did. Elisha received a double portion of his master's spirit and performed twice the number of miracles.

Although Elisha succeeded in his ministry, he was no mere clone of Elijah. Similarly, Joshua learned much from Moses, but fulfilled a role that was distinctly his own. The proof of good discipleship is not the creation of a carbon copy, but of an informed original. That's where discipling can fail and things can fossilize. God doesn't want fossils, though: he wants you to learn his ways both through your discipler and directly from his Spirit. You and God are a unique combination.

Discipleship is not only about passing on values and vision. People must also learn how to experience the power of the Holy Spirit. Elijah taught Elisha many things about God, but one thing captured Elisha's imagination more than any other. He had seen the Spirit of God resting on his master, and that, more than anything else, was what he wanted—in double measure.

Nothing could shake Elisha from his determination to experience this empowering. All the training in the world was no substitute for a personal endowment of power from on high. "If you see me when I am taken from you, it will be yours," replied Elijah (2 Kings 2:10), thereby prefiguring another who would ascend into heaven, leaving his disciples with the promise of power from the Holy Spirit.

Challenge of discipleship

The church must face the challenge of making disciples. Leaders, many excellent young men and women long to be discipled.

You may argue that you do not know how to make a disciple. Looking back, you do not remember anybody taking you under his wing. Somehow you made it on your own. Perhaps you do not know how to start. Perhaps you even feel that if anyone came really close to you he would discover your weaknesses and how you have failed the Lord in the past. It seems to me, though, that Elijah was a man just like you—and he trained a great disciple.

JONAH: A MAN WHO RAN FROM GOD

"The word of the Lord came to Jonah son of Amittai: 'Go to the great city of Nineveh and preach against it, because its wickedness has come up before me.' But Jonah ran away from the Lord."
— Jonah 1:1-3

Chapter 19

A PAROCHIAL PROPHET

We don't know much about the actual personalities of most Old Testament prophets, but God occasionally parts the curtains, permitting us to go behind the prophecies to meet the men themselves. So we see Moses agonizing in prayer; Jeremiah protesting, "Lord, I don't want to speak any more"; and Habakkuk wrestling over what is happening to his nation.

We would expect the book of Jonah to follow a similar pattern: lots of emphasis on the prophet's message with a few occasional glimpses of the man behind it. Not so here. The balance between "message and man" is completely reversed. Jonah's prophecy consists of eight words—half a Bible verse—and the rest of the four chapters unveil God's work in Jonah's life. The message which the Ninevites eventually hear represents only the tip of the iceberg. Action and attitudes outweigh words in this amazing drama.

Fact or fiction?

Some people say that the story of Jonah must be a fable. "It can't possibly be true," they declare. "The miracles are just too numerous and too incredible: the sudden storm; the fish swallowing Jonah; the prophet's survival in its stomach; his exit onto dry ground; national repentance; the plant that springs up one day and dies the next. It's all too much. Who could believe such a fantastic story?"

"Maybe," they suggest, "it's a parable, a learning aid concerning the people of Israel who disobeyed God and did not fulfill their calling to be a voice to the nations. God's judgment came through Babylon, which swallowed Israel and, after seventy years, vomited it up onto dry ground." Such interpretations fall apart when you begin to investigate further. Myths don't have fathers or addresses, and we read that Jonah was the son of Amittai (Jonah 1:1), that he came from Gath Hepher, and that he prophesied about the boundaries of Israel (2 Kings 14:25).

Jesus himself made it perfectly clear that Jonah was a real person by referring to the prophet in the same context as the historical Queen of Sheba, who came "to listen to Solomon's wisdom" (Luke 11:31). Jesus also endorsed the prophet's story by reminding his hearers that the men of Nineveh repented at the preaching of Jonah (Luke 11:32).

Gabriel came from heaven to tell us that "nothing is impossible with God," at whose command a virgin conceives, a blind man receives his sight, a rock produces water, the Red Sea parts, a storm is stilled, people are raised from the dead, and someone who is swallowed by a big fish lives to prophesy to a nation that repents and turns to God. As we follow Jonah's story we shall find that his very experiences contain a prophetic word for us today.

Don't disturb me

Jonah lived at the time of Jeroboam II (2 Kings 14:25). During that king's forty-one year reign Israel grew strong and prosperous. Indeed, no king after Solomon established such power as Jeroboam II, though he continued in the sins of Jeroboam I. In fact, Amos, the prophet who followed Jonah, prophesied against that whole generation for its greed and self-indulgence.

So life for Jonah must have been easygoing. A powerful king ruled over national prosperity. The nation's borders were extend-

ing as Jonah had prophesied; but the people, rich and unrepent-
ant, were still living sinfully. It was a dangerous time for a
prophet: the temptation to settle down and simply enjoy everything must have been great.

Into this sleepy, complacent atmosphere the word of God
suddenly came to Jonah: "Go to the great city of Nineveh" (Jonah
1:2). All the other Old Testament prophets were called to remind
Israel of its unique relationship with God and his law. Jonah,
however, received an alarming and unparalleled command—
"Go to the heathen."

Wake up!

Up to this point, the silence from heaven regarding the pagan
world might have suggested that God was indifferent to it. But
now, that silence was unexpectedly broken. Jonah, the parochial
prophet, suddenly heard God telling him to leave his sheltered
and comfortable life to cross the borders and preach God's
judgment to a people steeped in wickedness.

"The word of the Lord came to Jonah" (Jonah 1:1). A prophet
is essentially someone who hears from God, and Jonah, although
limited in his view, was a true prophet. He clearly heard from
God. But how did he react to the command to go to Nineveh?
Here he was, serving a local God, probably preoccupied with
temple rituals—sacrifices and offerings, special days, priestly
garments, pomegranates, and bells. Maybe he thought that God
was not concerned about anything else. So long as the temple
laws were followed to the letter, God would be happy.

I can imagine Jonah in the temple, meticulously examining the
priestly garments, nodding approvingly and saying, "Yes, hang-
ing on this robe are a bell, a tassel, and a pomegranate." And I
can imagine God calling, "Jonah!"

"Yes, Lord?"

"I want you to go to Nineveh."

"Yes, which Nineveh is that, Lord?"

"The large, famous city. I want you to go to that Nineveh."

"Why, Lord?"

"Because its wickedness has come up before me."

"Of course they're wicked—they're heathen!"

It must have been a staggering thought for Jonah—that God should care about heathen Nineveh, let alone want to say anything to it.

In times of spiritual awareness, the Israelites knew that they were called to be a light to the nations. Abraham had been told, "All peoples on earth will be blessed through you" (Gen. 12:3). And David, inspired by the Spirit, wrote, "Ask of me, and I will make the nations your inheritance, the ends of the earth your possession" (Ps. 2:8). This was a Messianic psalm, but David would have identified with it. He knew that God's purpose extended far beyond Israel to the nations of the world. Isaiah knew this too, since he made numerous references to God's worldwide rule.

When Israel was spiritually low, the people forgot the breadth of God's government and became introspective. So long as they kept their own house in order, all would be well. God would bless them. The heathen were "out there somewhere," excluded from the promises and of no importance whatsoever.

But one Old Testament king once glorified God, saying, "His dominion is an eternal dominion; his kingdom endures from generation to generation. All the peoples of the earth are regarded as nothing. He does as he pleases with the powers of heaven and the peoples of the earth. No one can hold back his hand or say to him: 'What have you done?'" (Dan. 4:34,35). Clearly, this man knew that God ruled the nations. But who made this tremendous statement about God? Nebuchadnezzar—a pagan king.

God also "anointed" Cyrus, and said of him, "He is my shepherd and will accomplish all that I please. . . . [He will] subdue nations before him. . . . I will give [him] the treasures of darkness, riches stored in secret places. . . " (Isa. 44:28; 45:1,3). Hearing these words, the average Jew would have protested, "Cyrus is a heathen king; he doesn't know God. He can't be included in God's plans." But God had other ideas.

He had these "other ideas" for the Messiah, too! His prophetic word to his Son was, "It is too small a thing for you to be my servant to restore the tribes of Jacob. . . . I will also make you a light for the Gentiles, that you may bring my salvation to the ends of the earth" (Isa. 49:6). God knew that the Jewish nation was backslidden and desperately needed restoration, but "Operation Israel" was too small a project for Jesus! God wanted his Son to reach not a little corner of the world but all of it.

Get a bigger vision

Today God would say, "It is too small a thing for you to give yourself only to the restoration of the church in your small corner of the world. I call you to be a light to the nations, that you may bring my salvation to the ends of the earth. Don't be so preoccupied with the 10 percent when the 90 percent outside need to hear my word."

Restoring the church is a worthy cause, but beware of introspection. "We had a beautiful time of worship this week. The music is coming together nicely. People are really opening up to one another now. Lots of hurts are getting healed." Rejoice that your church is no longer boring. Rejoice when God moves among you. Rejoice when relations, neighbors, and friends are saved. But don't become so totally preoccupied with the scrutiny of bells, tassels, and pomegranates that you forget God's vision for the nations.

Doubtless many aspects of New Testament church life still need to be recovered, but do not grow stagnant and inward-looking, forgetting God's great plan to reach all the families of the earth. It is too small a thing to concentrate exclusively on restoring your little patch when God wants to lift your head, show you the harvest field, and send you to dying sinners with his glorious message of salvation.

Jesus is not just head over the church, be it local or universal. He said, "All authority in heaven and on earth has been given to me" (Matt. 28:18). He is head over all things (Eph. 1:10). He is ruling as king over every nation at this very minute.

Do not think, "That's a Moslem nation; that's a Hindu nation; that's a Communist nation; and of course we're a backslidden Christian nation." God thinks differently. While looking down on Nineveh he did not say, "I'd be concerned if such wickedness were apparent in Judea, but what more can you expect from heathen Nineveh?" Rather, when God saw how wicked the Ninevites were, he could not stand it and sent someone to warn them.

When God looks down on any nation, he does not simply view it as "heathen" and quickly put it out of his mind. He sees the terrible contrast between rich and poor in India. He watches their idol worship. He observes China's dreadful policy of infanticide and its soaring abortion rate. He knows about nations where people are torn away from their families, unjustly beaten and thrown into prison. He sees the ravages of AIDS in Africa. America's battered children and increasing crime rate do not go unnoticed.

God is saying, "Go!" That's what you have been called to do: to reach the nations—all of them! Jesus said, "This gospel of the kingdom will be preached in the whole world as a testimony to all nations" (Matt. 24:14). He said that we would be hated by all nations (Matt.24:9) and that one day all the nations will be gathered before him (Matt. 25:32).

You could spend hours trying to work out the intricacies of various doctrines or church practices in an attempt to get all the details absolutely right. Indeed, there will always be something not quite perfect that will need your attention. But what about the world? The restoration of the church has consumed you, but now a new day is dawning. Whereas the word "church" has stirred you, let the word "nations" burn in your heart—because it's time to look at the harvest fields and it's time to go.

CHAPTER 20

HOW CAN YOU SLEEP?

Was God's concern for heathen Nineveh too much for narrow-minded Jonah to take? Was the prophet alarmed at the prospect of preaching his uncomfortable message to the heathen? Whatever he felt, he ran. God had plans for Jonah, "but Jonah ran . . . " (Jonah 1:3). I wonder how often this is the case with us. God had plans for Mike, but Mike ran. . . . God had plans for Anne, but Anne ran. . . .

Jonah ran from the presence of the Lord. Many people wonder if it is possible to run from God's presence. I think the answer is both yes and no. No, declares David in Psalm 139: "Where can I go from your Spirit? Where can I flee from your presence? If I go up to the heavens, you are there; if I make my bed in the depths, you are there" (vv. 7,8). "I cannot run away from you" he says. "It doesn't matter where I go, I cannot escape from your presence." Yes, he says in Psalm 51: "Do not cast me from your presence" (v. 11).

Some Christians would simply quote the doctrine that God is omnipresent. Therefore, since God is everywhere, it is impossible to flee from his presence. So when they hear someone say enthusiastically, "We really felt the presence of God in the meeting this morning," they react matter-of-factly, "Well, he's always there." Such dry application of doctrine provides a snare for the evangelical church, robbing us as it does of the anticipation of feeling God's presence.

The mystery is that we can experience both God's closeness and his withdrawal. One of Jesus' names is Immanuel, which means "God with us," but he did not say, "You will always feel my presence." He promised simply, "I am with you always" (Matt. 28:20, NKJV).

Moses said to God, "If your presence does not go with us, do not send us up from here" (Ex. 33:15). He was not careless about the presence of God. He did not put his confidence in a passionless statement, "God is everywhere." In fact, God had just said that he would go with the people (33:14). But Moses wanted God to know how determined he was that his presence be manifest among them.

When Jonah fled from the presence of the Lord, he was escaping from the revealed will of God and was forsaking the enjoyment of his fellowship.

Amazing coincidence

The prophet went down to Joppa in search of a ship bound for Tarshish. On finding one he probably thought, "It was meant for me. What an extraordinary coincidence! What proof that I'm not off course after all." After paying his fare he went aboard. He failed to realize that the devil could have supplied a whole fleet of ships headed for Tarshish.

If Jonah had been listening to his conscience, he would have heard the words, "You shouldn't be going this way." But he chose instead to take note of circumstances, and they seemed to suggest that he wasn't on such a perilous course at all.

When you are determined to go your own way, not only do you turn your back on the revealed will of God, you also become vulnerable to putting significance in coincidences. "I know my girlfriend isn't a Christian yet," you say, "but look at how we were thrown together. We were obviously meant for each other." "My boss wants me involved in that business deal. I know it's shady, but it's come across my path in such an amazing way."

Unlike Jonah, Paul was determined to do the will of God and therefore experienced his guidance. On one occasion he wanted to preach in Asia, but the Holy Spirit stopped him (Acts 16:6). A little later he tried to enter Bithynia, but again the Spirit said no (Acts 16:7) and drew him back into God's will.

Rather than say naively, "It just opened up to me," begin to listen attentively to your conscience. Learn to detect the voice that says, "Keep away from that place," "Avoid a relationship with that person," "Don't get into that," "The Spirit isn't leading you there." Beware of "finding a ship." It will only take you on a journey that you will later regret.

The sleeping prophet

God had told Jonah, "Go to Nineveh." Jonah responded, "Not likely! I'm off to Tarshish." Having secured his passage, he went below deck and promptly fell asleep.

Tiredness can be perfectly healthy, the natural result of hard work. At the end of a particularly demanding day, we fall into bed and sleep. That's good and healthy. But we can also experience a tiredness that is not healthy, a sleep that says, "I can't face reality anymore. I can't cope with the responsibility." Jonah had already run away physically. Now he was running away mentally. He lost all sense of purpose and along with it, all sense of urgency. Dejected and weary, he crawled below deck and fell asleep.

In the Garden of Gethsemane Jesus told the disciples to watch and pray, but they fell asleep. Probably they had simply had enough. Jesus had warned them about his death, and now the pressures were mounting. They must have thought, "We're weary of all this. What's the point? If Jesus dies what's going to happen to us? It's just too much for us to cope with." So they switched off and fell asleep.

There's a tiredness which is based on escapism, one which turns on the television and says, "I don't care what rubbish is on. I can't bear facing reality." And when the head hits the pillow at night there's a big sigh of relief: "I can turn my back on it! I can sleep!"

How many Christians suffer from lethargy and general aimlessness? We have a glorious commission—to tell the world about Jesus—but how often do we give the impression of having a vital sense of destiny? Forgetting God's command to reach the nations, we simply adopt our own plans. We soon lose our sense of direction, get bored, and "fall asleep." So the world regards Christians as sleepy and irrelevant rather than provocative or prophetic.

Storm-tossed world

Suddenly a violent storm engulfed Jonah's ship. Panic gripped the terrified sailors, who cried out to their gods to save them. Fearing that they would capsize in the gigantic waves, all hands were ordered on deck, and cargo was frantically thrown overboard.

Today the world is confronted by many terrible storms: moral storms, economic storms, ecological storms. People are tossed about by countless fears, and countless social needs scream out for answers. Though modern man is better educated and informed than ever, he still feels overwhelmed by the enormity of the world's problems. Just as Jonah's companions called on their various gods, so society cries out to humanism, communism, materialism. But once tried, they are all found wanting. Now some are turning to occult or eastern religions—Islam, Hinduism, Hare Krishna, Mormonism, spiritualism, and so on. Not knowing who has the answer, each calls on his own "god" for help.

Jonah's shipmates did not realize it, but the one man who knew how to stop the storm was asleep. "How can you sleep?" the ship's captain asked him. "Get up and call on your god." Everybody else was doing what they could—praying to their gods, bailing out water, discarding cargo—but Jonah only slept. "Why don't you join us in what we are doing?" Backslidden

Christians are often faced with the same sort of question by well-meaning friends and colleagues, but it is pointless trying to "bail out the water" when you, like Jonah, know the reason for the storm.

The moment Jonah was cornered he knew more about the weather conditions in the Mediterranean than the entire meteorological office of his day! The sailors may have calculated that certain winds had reacted with high and low pressure areas, and the result was a storm. But this backslider knew exactly what was happening. "It's me," he told them. "I'm the cause."

Backsliders who have been apprehended by God often know more about the situation than anyone else, whatever the specialists may say. The backslider on the verge of bankruptcy can call in an expert to help him save his business. The man might suggest, "Well, you should enlarge here and develop there, and you should work at cash flow. Then you'll probably break through." Or to help save his crumbling marriage, he may consult a marriage guidance counselor, who suggests, "If you stop doing this and do that instead, you'll have a far better chance of pulling your marriage together." But in his heart the backslider thinks, "No. It isn't any of that. God's after me."

God has a heart for backsliders. He closes in on them, whispering through the storms, "I'm after you. You've run away from me, but I love you, and I haven't finished with you. I want you back with me again."

Awake, O Zion!

But God doesn't want only to shake individuals. He wants to shake the church.

The church is God's messenger to a storm-tossed world. She holds the keys to the nations. She knows the answers that everybody needs to hear. How can the church sleep while the world is agonizing with such colossal pressures? How can she drift while people's hearts are failing on every side? Suicides, drug addiction, mindless brutality, abused children, elderly people terrified to answer their doorbells at night—what a world we live in. How can the church, God's prophetic voice to the nations, become so purposeless and fall asleep?

When the church forgets her calling, when she turns her back on her obligation to the lost, she suffers a total loss of identity. Bake sales and bazaars are hardly the mark of a prophetic people who bring God's answers into the turmoil of our generation! Christians who rejoice only in inward-looking ministry are barely more relevant. God wants to shake us out of our complacency. If the unsaved really knew what we know about heaven and hell and free salvation through Christ, they would say to us, "How can you sleep?" We must wake up to our identity and our calling. We must be restored to a true fear of the Lord.

As soon as Jonah admitted his identity and acknowledged that he worshiped God, reality broke in. Until then he had been running away, but once he affirmed his fear of God, the mystery was solved. Jonah's admission, "I fear God," had a startling effect on the sailors. They were terrified and began to cry out to God and offer him sacrifices. That's how revival breaks out. When the wayward church wakes up to its true identity and declares, "I fear God," people are frightened and begin to pray and seek him for themselves. This is the real distinction between organized evangelism and revival. Revival begins in the church when God's people genuinely reaffirm their fear of the Lord and reclaim a right relationship with him. The repercussions have a powerful effect on society.

Personally identified with God's purposes

In the face of Jonah's disobedience, God would have been justified in saying, "Jonah has deserted his post and cannot be trusted. I'll just let him go. Amos is much more reliable. Amos, you go instead!"

But although God could have turned to Amos, he did not, because he had chosen Jonah. Having started a great work in this wayward prophet, God was committed to completing it. He loved Jonah and stood by him, just as he had stood by Abraham,

Moses, David, Elijah, Peter, and others when they drifted from his plans. God's faithfulness to backsliders is amazing. His covenant love extends beyond our wildest dreams.

Just as God's purpose was personified in Jonah, so his purpose is wrapped up in the church. He sees the church's faults and failings, but he will never abandon it. Do you think God will say, "I've had about as much as I can take from the church! I think I'll scrap it and look somewhere else for support. Maybe I'll ask a couple of million angels to help me out. They'd be much more reliable." No: God chose the church, and he will complete his work through the church. We will reach all the nations. God has said so, and he is 100 percent committed to us.

God was sickened by the wickedness of Nineveh. The people's sin angered him. He could have destroyed the city, but he longed to show compassion, to be merciful, to offer the Ninevites the opportunity to repent.

Today God wants you to share his anguish. "Look at those huge cities: New York, Chicago, Los Angeles, and all the rest," he would say. "Their wickedness has come up before me, and I'm angry at their sin, but I love the people and long to show them compassion and mercy. Take the gospel to them. I want to display my love and power in your cities, to give them the opportunity to repent."

Are you personally obeying God in this great commission, or have you fallen asleep? The heathen captain asked the backslidden prophet, "How can you sleep? Have you noticed the terrifying storm? Have you seen the size of the waves? Don't you realize we will all perish?" Death and destruction seemed to be closing in on his frail life, and God's servant, who knew the answers, was asleep.

God wants you not only to know about the great work he is planning for the nations, he wants you to be involved in it. Don't go running in the wrong direction, spending your resources on the wrong things and falling asleep to the world's need as though it did not affect you. God will send the storm and shake you until you get back on course, until you are caught up with him in his worldwide purpose, until you get up on your feet, acknowledge your waywardness, and cry out, "Lord, I'm coming back! I'm ready to follow your command."

CHAPTER 21

A SECOND CHANCE

"The word of the Lord came to Jonah a second time" (Jonah 3:1). What a glorious statement. Many famous Bible characters could stand and tell us about God's wonderful mercy: how he came to them again, the second time.

Abraham could give his testimony, followed by Moses, David, Elijah, Peter, and others—all stepping forward to say that the Lord does give you a second chance. When you think you have totally disqualified yourself, God draws near and returns you to the path of his original purpose. What a merciful God we serve. His patience and kindness are unfathomable.

But before God spoke to Jonah a second time, Jonah did some speaking of his own. In fact he did some serious praying.

Floundering around in the water, sinking like a stone, he suddenly found himself inside a huge fish. What else could he have prayed?

"Help!" That's where you start. You don't begin by trying to work out exactly how God might want to be addressed—"I beseech thee, almighty God, creator of the universe. . . ." You don't begin by reviewing your own unworthiness and the various sins you've committed since you drifted away. There are times when urgency totally eclipses formality.

You may be wondering, "How am I going to come back to God? The implications are frightening, and I don't know if I can face them." Like Jonah, you might feel, "If I come back to God, I will have to face up to doing what he was telling me to do."

But don't let that deter you. Be honest with yourself and tell God exactly how you feel. Tell him, "I'm afraid of what you might ask of me, but I want to get back into your will. Help me, Lord."

"Help!" is a cry God cannot ignore. You could be restored to God as you read this chapter. Why don't you cry to him for help even now, at this very moment?

Jonah believed in a sovereign God

Jonah acknowledged that God was behind everything that was happening to him. "You hurled me into the deep," he said. "All your waves and breakers swept over me" (Jonah 2:3). He knew that he was God's captive, that God had been pursuing him.

When we become children of God, we are never free agents again. We are never finally at the mercy of circumstance. We have been bought with a price; we belong to God; we are in his hand. He is our new master, and we are his captives.

In his letter to Philemon, Paul did not begin, "Paul, a prisoner of the Roman guard. . ."; he wrote, "Paul, a prisoner of Christ Jesus" (Philem. 1:1). In his letter to the Romans, he did not say, "Try hard to be slaves of God." He said, "[you] have become slaves to righteousness. . . [you] have become slaves to God" (Rom. 6:18,22).

The fact is that as a Christian, you are Christ's slave. That's why you feel so desperately uncomfortable when you stray from the will of God. Something in your heart says, "You really shouldn't be doing this." The voice belongs to your new owner. He troubles your conscience. It's hard going.

I once knew a man who drifted far away from God. He got into an adulterous relationship and refused to face up to his rebellion.

Then one day he had a heart attack. Lying in the ambulance he overheard the paramedics saying, "I don't know if he'll still be alive by the time we get him to the hospital." As he lay there, helpless, he cried out, "God save me!" Though backslidden, like Jonah, he knew enough about God and his mercy to call on him again.

Banished

As he continued his prayer, Jonah said, "You have expelled me from your sight" (Jonah 2:4). Jonah felt as though he had been forsaken.

"Banished," the New International Version translates it. Imagine a medieval knight discovered in a plot against the king. He stands before the king who passes sentence: "You are banished from the land." Slowly, the full horror of banishment dawns on him. That's how Jonah felt—not just judged but banished, outside, away from where he ought to be. He did not argue against his sentence. On the contrary, he acknowledged the justice of it.

Hope restored

In the midst of his turmoil, in spite of his feelings of rejection by God, he declared, "Yet I will look again toward your holy temple" (Jonah 2:4). What did he mean? He was really saying, "I remember your covenant promise." Into his unrelieved darkness came a ray of light. God had sealed a promise with his covenant people.

Solomon's temple was built in obedience to the command of God. When it was completed, Solomon gathered all Israel together and prayed, "O Lord my God. . . . May your eyes be open toward this temple day and night. . . because your people have sinned against you, and when they pray toward this place and confess your name and turn from their sin because you have afflicted them, then hear from heaven and forgive the sin of your servants, your people Israel" (2 Chron. 6:19,20,26,27). God heard his prayer. He filled the temple with his glory and made a covenant with Solomon to listen and respond when anyone repented and prayed toward the temple.

Jonah looked back into the dim past and recalled Solomon's prayer and God's answer. "I've been expelled," he thought to himself, "But there was a promise, wasn't there? Surely if I look again to the holy temple, you will hear me. You will answer me. You said you would."

Some Christians say, "I used to be a servant of God, but I've cut myself off from him." But don't you remember that somewhere in the distant past there was a covenant? Search your memory. Weren't there promises? Didn't God say, "I have loved you with an everlasting love" (Jer. 31:3)? Didn't he say, "Never will I leave you; never will I forsake you" (Heb. 13:5)? Didn't he promise that if we confessed our sins, Jesus would forgive us?

No one needs to remain under a cloud of condemnation. Jonah looked to the temple; you can look to Jesus. You are not worthy, but he is. Cry out to him, "Lord, you promised. You promised you'd always love me and never leave me. You promised that if I confessed my sin you would be faithful and just to forgive my sin and cleanse me from all unrighteousness. Lord, I claim your promise. I repent, and I return to you now with all my heart."

Fulfilling your vow

Jonah also added, "What I have vowed I will make good" (Jonah 2:9). Now that he was returning to God, Jonah knew that he must also return to his vow and to the word that God had originally given. Unless you are willing to return and be totally obedient to the word God originally gave you, and to fulfill your commitment to him as Lord, you are not truly repenting.

Have you made a vow to God? Did you once promise him something? Maybe earlier in your Christian life you responded to God's call and said, "You can count on me!" But time has passed, and you have lost the zeal you once had. You have become preoccupied with your career, your family, your hobbies. Your vow is almost forgotten.

Maybe you made a different sort of commitment to God: "I will sort out my financial affairs, Lord. I'll pay the tax I haven't declared and start tithing." "I won't indulge in that bad habit any more." "I won't get involved in a relationship with that person. I know it's not right." But you haven't done what you said you would. For one reason or another, you haven't fulfilled the vow.

Sometimes people make vows when they are caught in a crisis. "Oh, God!" they cry out, "Help me! Get me out of this and I promise you I'll. . . ." And God graciously steps in and rescues them. They are delighted. "Thank you, Lord!" they say. "I'm so grateful." Then time passes, and the vow slowly fades from memory until it is viewed as little more than a rash comment made on the spur of a difficult moment.

"I can't fulfill that promise now," some people say to God. "I just can't face it. Besides, I really don't think I've got the resources any more. I had them when I made the promise, but now things have changed. It's different. You understand, Lord, don't you?"

Yes, he understands. But he has not said, "All right, forget the vow." We can try by various means to relinquish our responsibility, but God has not released us from it. "The vow is still outstanding," he says. "I'm waiting for you to fulfill it, and I'll be there to help you. Don't back away any more. Do what you promised you would, and I will restore you—completely."

The Bible tells us, "When you make a vow to God, do not delay in fulfilling it. He has no pleasure in fools; fulfill your vow. It is better not to vow than to make a vow and not fulfill it" (Ecc. 5:4,5).

God wants you to come back to the root of your problem. He longs to hear from you the words of the psalmist, "I will. . . fulfill my vows to you—vows my lips promised and my mouth spoke when I was in trouble" (Ps. 66:13,14). You may want God to work on your terms, but he wants to lift your standards to his. "Come back into my will," he says. "Come back and fulfill the original vision. It's the only way forward."

Jonah—far removed from God's will, alone, tired, and miserable—prayed, "What I have vowed I will make good." In that moment, as if a severed electric cable had been rejoined to its source, there was light, power, revelation, and a shout of assurance, "Salvation comes from the Lord" (Jonah 2:9). His declaration triggered an immediate response in heaven: "And the Lord commanded the fish, and it vomited Jonah onto dry land" (Jonah 2:10).

Release

"The Lord commanded the fish." Amazing. And fish are not the only things God can command. "Aaron's staff, become a snake!" he ordered. "Sand, turn into gnats!" "Locusts, gather your friends and populate Egypt!" "Red Sea, open up!" "Walls of Jericho, fall!" "Lions, spare Daniel!" "Fire, don't touch those three men!" Is there anything he cannot command? No, nothing. Seas open, walls fall, lions shut their mouths, fire is harmless, and even death yields its captives. At his word everything obeys. Every confinement ceases. You cannot be entrapped by anything that will refuse to obey God's command.

Jonah was imprisoned by his circumstances, but God's command released him. "I feel so trapped by my situation," you may say. But God can change it overnight. "Job situation, change!" he can order. "Money, get into her bank account!" "Managing director, promote him to that position!" God is far greater than our circumstances. At any time he can command our "fish," "Enough! Let him go!" And the fish will cough us up—not back into the sea, but onto dry land.

The Bible tells us, "For you, O God, tested us; you refined us like silver. You brought us into prison and laid burdens on our backs. You let men ride over our heads; we went through fire and water, but you brought us to a place of abundance" (Ps. 66:10-12). God takes his people through difficult circumstances, not because he wants to hurt them, but because he wants to strengthen them and make them more effective. React positively to confinement, and you will one day, like imprisoned and forgotten Joseph, find yourself suddenly released onto dry ground and into great things.

A second time

At last Jonah was on dry ground, delivered, delighted, but probably disqualified—or was he? No! Here we find those wonderful words, "The word of the Lord came to Jonah a second time" (Jonah 3:1). What a glorious statement. We may have written Jonah off; he might even have disqualified himself. But God did not abandon him: he brought his prophet right back into his original plans, back to where he had left off.

Throughout Scripture we read of scarred people whom God had chosen and who heard from him a second time. Abraham, unable to wait for God to give him a child by his wife Sarah, produced a son through her maid, Hagar. "That's it," we would have said. "He's blown it. No chance of God using him now." But after thirteen years, Abraham heard God's voice again: "Your wife Sarah will bear you a son" (Gen. 17:19). And a year later the promise was fulfilled.

Then there was Moses. "I'll deliver Israel," he said, then killed an Egyptian and ran for his life. "He's blown his chances of rescuing the nation now," we assume. But no. Forty years later God called him again, and Moses brought the Israelites out of bondage just as God had intended. And what about David, the man after God's own heart? He committed adultery and as good as murdered the woman's husband. Was he pushed to one side? No. He went through terrible conviction of sin, but God forgave him and reinstated him as king.

Peter cursed and swore that he didn't know Jesus, but he was not overlooked from that time on. God's word came to Peter a second time: "Do you love me?" And on the day of Pentecost, who was it standing there preaching the gospel, to which 3,000 people responded?

God's grace says, "My dear child, put behind you what you've done and go on as though it never happened. Come back—not to a different word, but back to my original word to you. I will gladly pick you up and reinstate you to my original purpose. That's what I've wanted all along."

What was Jonah's response? He "went according to the word of the Lord." That's what God wants from us—to go according to his word. Have you messed up your marriage? Is your business on shaky ground? Have you been resisting God in your spiritual life? Get back into line with the word of God. Jonah did. Will you?

CHAPTER 22

A HAPPY ENDING?

It was electrifying. The weird figure stood in the city center, his skin strangely colored, his clothes worn and dusty, and began to shout, "Nineveh, hear me! In forty days you will be overturned!" No explanation, no credentials presented, no alternatives offered. Why should the people heed him at all? Yet they did.

The impact of Jonah's words was astounding. Hearing the news of impending doom, the ordinary citizens were first to respond. The entire population declared a fast and put on sackcloth. Then the king learned there was something happening among his people, and he, too, humbled himself. This large-scale repentance was not just outwardly impressive, it was genuine. The Ninevites were not merely observing religious practices, they were actually turning from their evil ways (Jonah 3:10) and completely changing their lifestyle.

Here is a classic example of a genuine spiritual revival that eventually changes society itself. Bills passed in Congress will not ultimately change society. You cannot legislate a nation into righteousness. Only a powerful outpouring of the Holy Spirit in revival can change the moral climate of a nation.

When that change takes place, those in authority become

aware of a new morality emerging, and in the wake of such a visitation genuine reformers are raised up. Holiness begins to be seen in our schools, shops, factories, and offices. And as moral standards begin to rise at the grass-roots level, so the government will adjust the laws of the land to reflect new national attitudes.

We must still pray for our rulers and write to our congressmen about specific issues, but note that in Nineveh, the national transformation started among the people. Wesley saw a similar pattern in England in his day. Genuine revival is a sovereign intervention of God. Meanwhile, we must preach the gospel where we are—among ordinary people in our neighborhoods, workplaces, schools. As individuals repent, they will, in turn, influence the nation.

So it was that all of Nineveh repented, from the least to the greatest. Three thousand converts on the day of Pentecost was amazing, but look at this. In all church history I have never heard of such a sweeping revival as there was in Nineveh. What a glorious climax to an extraordinary story. Jonah had learned his lessons, and a mighty revival took place.

At this point, we would expect the curtain to fall and thunderous applause to break out among God's people. "That must be the final scene," we would think as we glanced quickly down the program:

Act 1

Scene 1:   God speaks to Jonah

Scene 2:   Jonah runs away

Act 2

Scene 1:   Jonah is chastised

Scene 2:   Jonah repents

Scene 3:   Jonah is restored

Act 3

Scene 1:   Jonah obeys

Scene 2:   Jonah is overwhelmingly successful

"Terrific," we think. "What a magnificent story! Now, where's my coat?" The applause subsides and we get up to leave, when suddenly the curtain rises. "What's this?" we say, startled. We look again at the program, turn over to the back page and read:

Act 4

Scene 1:   God speaks to Jonah again

On the stage sits a solitary figure. The Ninevites have all gone, and Jonah is left alone with his God. The curtain has fallen on the story but has risen again to reveal the heart of the prophet.

So the book of Jonah ends not with the triumphant climax of chapter three, but with chapter four. This chapter will appear at the end of every one of our life stories. It begins when the final curtain has dropped on your earthly life, when people have held your funeral service and applauded you for your great contribution to the world. Then the curtain will rise again, and you will be alone before God, and he will look into your heart.

Behind the scenes

Most people judge by what they see in a person. God is more impressed by the unseen. Samuel received a gentle rebuke from God when he was trying to discover which of Jesse's sons he should anoint as king. "You're looking at his stature," said God, "but the Lord looks at the heart." Men might be very impressed by actions, but God is far more interested in what goes on behind them. We read, "The Lord is a God who knows, and by him deeds are weighed" (1 Sam. 2:3) and, "All a man's ways seem innocent to him, but motives are weighed by the Lord" (Prov. 16:2).

When you have come to the end of your life, you will receive an appraisal based not so much on your achievements as on your motivation. You might remind God, "I was involved in the conversion of over a hundred and twenty thousand. You must be impressed by that. It was a tremendous revival. That's what you were looking for, wasn't it? So now the curtain can fall."

No. God is looking for more than success. He is interested in the secret motivation of his individual servants. Your work "will be shown for what it is, because the Day will bring it to light. It will be revealed with fire, and the fire will test the quality of each man's work. If what he has built survives, he will receive his reward. If it is burned up, he will suffer loss; he himself will be saved, but only as one escaping through the flames" (1 Cor. 3:13-15).

This passage is not talking about salvation, which is a work of grace through faith in Christ. Here the emphasis is on reward for ministry. It concerns things which are left standing after God has searched your motivation. Some will suffer loss, while others will be rewarded. But for all of us, there will inevitably be a "chapter four"—when the crowds have gone, with no one around to be impressed by externals, when it's just God and you; and he will look right into your heart.

The apostle Paul was not concerned by what people thought of him. He said, "I care very little if I am judged by you or by any human court; indeed, I do not even judge myself. My conscience is clear, but that does not make me innocent. It is the Lord who judges me" (1 Cor. 4:3,4). Although Paul felt that his conscience was clear, he did not finally even trust those feelings; he realized that God knew better than his conscience. "He will bring to light what is hidden in darkness and will expose the motives of men's hearts. At that time each will receive his praise from God" (1 Cor. 4:5).

You can have a great career, you can bask in the praise of men, but nothing will ever compare with the "Well done" that comes from God. Imagine being praised by God! Imagine hearing him say to you, "Well done! I'm really pleased with you." Surely that prospect must be one of the most exciting in all the universe! Surely it is your highest desire: to live to please God and, at the end, to hear his words, "Well done, good and faithful servant. . . . Come and share your master's happiness" (Matt. 25:21).

I have had some exciting days. I remember the day I was saved. I remember the day I got married and the days when our children were born. I remember tremendous, exciting days in my life, days to treasure. But there will never, never be a day to compare with the day when I receive my praise from God, when I hear him say, "Well done."

When the curtain rises for the last time, there will be a great turning around. Jesus said, "The last will be first, and the first will be last" (Matt. 20:16). The people who wanted and received their acclamation from men will be disappointed when they meet God. But those whose hearts were truly seeking after righteousness will be rewarded.

God is interested in hearts, and no one except God knew what was going on in Jonah's heart. When Jonah reached his chapter four, God confronted him, saying, "I want to talk to you about your motivation. I want to reveal what is hidden inside." And so the spotlight goes on, and we are allowed to eavesdrop on this extraordinary encounter.

Self-justification

"But Jonah was greatly displeased and very angry" (Jonah 4:1). How sad that Jonah's chapter four should begin this way. He had just witnessed a great revival, a mighty turning to God. We would expect the prophet to be rejoicing, ecstatic at the people's response to God's word, yet Jonah's reaction reflected not joy but hostility.

"Isn't this what I said while I was still at home?" he blurted out. "Before I left I said you would do this. That's why I ran away. I know that you're a compassionate God, and I told you that you would let them off. I was right in the first place."

The Ninevites had repented, but Jonah had not. He had not changed his mind about anything. "Get me out of this fish," he had cried to God when he was in distress. But when God released him, he did not change inwardly. He had not come into line with God's view at all. All this wayward prophet wanted to do was justify himself.

You can have the same experience. "God, please get me out of this!" He releases you only to discover that your repentance is superficial. It is not enough for you to feel the pressure of a situation. You must repent, change your heart, and say, "Lord, you spoke to me clearly. I used to justify myself, but I'm not going to argue any more. I won't be like Jonah—out of the pressure but inwardly unchanged. You want me to be different deep inside. When I cried to you, it was the beginning of a consistent change in my life."

Self-importance

"In forty days you're all going to be condemned," Jonah told the Ninevites, but in his heart he knew that God would show them mercy. Jonah had no love for them. He was more concerned about his own self-importance. At the same time he was declaring "You're all going to die," he was thinking, "What's going to happen to my prophetic ministry when the people don't die?" This man was more concerned with the vindication of his prophetic gift than with the overall purpose of God. "My ministry! My ministry! I must protect my ministry!"

The apostle Paul was thrown in prison, and from there he wrote to the Philippians: "Some preach Christ out of envy and rivalry, but others out of goodwill. . . . But what does it matter? The important thing is that in every way, whether from false motives or true, Christ is preached. And because of this I rejoice" (Phil. 1:15,18). Paul did not feel remotely threatened by others who were preaching the gospel outside his prison walls. He recognized that God's purpose was far bigger than his personal ministry.

We have to choose whether we adopt a "Jonah attitude" or a "Paul attitude." The Jonahs among us complain, "I've got a really important ministry but there's no room for it here. I'm fed up waiting to get my voice heard, so I think I'll leave the church." But the Pauls among us say, "Lord, I know you're accomplishing your purposes here. I want to be part of this, so I'll just serve you wherever I can. I know you will open doors for me if I'm not so much taken up with my ministry as I am with you."

Once Jonah had given God's message to the Ninevites, he sat down outside the city and said to himself, "Okay, let's see what happens to them." How cold and unfeeling can you get? This man had just been walking through a vast condemned city. He had passed children in the streets, men and women going about their daily business, cripples and beggars. "Forty more days, and that's it for you!" he had declared in his professional prophetic way. There is no hint of compassion, no saying to himself, "They've only got forty days. I must get among them. Perhaps I can do something to help."

When Jesus came to be baptized, John the Baptist protested, "I need to be baptized by you, and do you come to me?" (Matt. 3:14). But Jesus wanted to identify with us. He wanted to be the sort of friend who would not just stand and watch us suffer God's imminent condemnation. So he went through our experiences with us. He walked alongside us, served us, and died for us. That was his way.

It was not, however, Jonah's way. Once Jonah had delivered his message, he shot off, then sat and waited for the fire to fall.

Self-importance is a terrible trap. It is easy to become so wrapped up in "my ministry" that you become indifferent to God's purposes. "We had a wonderful home group meeting last night," you think to yourself. "People really appreciated that message I shared. I'm beginning to shine. Have I got an anointing?" This is so dangerous, so frightening. And it is so sad that Jonah escaped the fish only to plunge into the jaws of self-centeredness.

Self-pity

Jonah made himself a shelter, and God caused a plant to grow over his head to ease his discomfort. Jonah was "very happy about the vine" (Jonah 4:6). "Super," he said to himself, "a vine! The sun's off me—marvelous!" Amazing, isn't it? Jonah was more concerned about a plant than about the whole city. And when the vine died and the sun blazed down on him, he fell again into depression and wanted to die.

This man was like a yo-yo. One minute he was up, the next he was down. While he was inside the fish he cried out, "Help, Lord! Save me!" Then, when God rescued him, he said, "I want to die." When the vine grew over him, he was happy, but when it withered, he withered along with it. Talk about living by your emotions.

We can be the same way. We cry out, "Lord, just get me out of this. I'll be obedient to you. I'll change." And God is merciful. He releases us and for a while we are very happy. But after a few weeks other pressures come and we begin to lapse into self-pity. "Why did you command the worm to eat my vine?" we protest to God. "It isn't fair. You don't love me any more. I think I'll leave the church."

What pathetic attitudes we sometimes adopt. How will we feel when we meet the Lord, and he uncovers them all? Happily for Jonah, his feet were still on the earth. He was not yet meeting with God as his ultimate judge, but as one who was still showing him amazing mercy and trying to win his heart. God certainly strives with his children, but in the end, we shall all have to account for what we did on earth.

CHAPTER 23

ALONE WITH GOD

Jonah destroys all our theories that God uses only the totally sanctified to fulfill his greatest purposes. Jonah's heart wasn't right, and neither was Samson's, but both moved powerfully.

God uses unsanctified servants

Church history is littered with people who had powerful ministries but who did not live as God intended. Some preached to thousands and even saw many saved, healed, and delivered while behind the scenes they were indulging in all manner of questionable activities.

When character declines, anointing does not necessarily cease immediately. Church history seems to indicate that for a while, anointing outlasts character until God sighs, "Enough!" Samson discovered this to his terrible cost. Beware of being impressed by externals. Just because someone is powerful in public does not necessarily mean that he is pleasing God in private.

God responds mercifully to inadequate repentance

Well might we ask, "Lord, why did you ever take Jonah out of the fish? He's a dreadful character. You should at least have left him in there a bit longer." But that's the wonder of God. He knew that Jonah's repentance wasn't complete, but still had mercy on him. "That's enough. I'll release him now, but I haven't finished with him yet."

Maybe God has recently rescued you from some great crisis and given you a great new sense of fulfillment and usefulness. Fine. But don't think that you are now the completed saint. Your heart may not yet be absolutely right. God has displayed his amazing grace to you, but he wants to take you still further.

A lady I once knew often said to me, "Every time you preach, God speaks to me about my smoking habit." The issue became an obsession. "I feel so condemned," she told me, "but I can't give it up." One day, I said to her, "Actually, God wants to speak to you about a lot of things. It's just that whatever message you hear, you relate it to smoking."

Soon after this, she broke her habit. "That's it!" she thought. "I've done it! I'm through!" But she wasn't. True, she had conquered smoking, but she suddenly realized that this small part of her life had assumed huge proportions in her mind. Once the clouds of smoke had lifted she saw more clearly that God had much more to say to her. She was not sanctified overnight. God had not finished with her.

Some people have taught that sanctification is there for the asking. You can read about "The Higher Life" or "The Secret Way," where you are encouraged to just "let go and let God." You say to him, "I've received justification by faith. Now I receive sanctification by faith. Hallelujah! I'm through! Sanctified!"

But the Bible doesn't teach sanctification by faith. It is not an instantaneous experience. God did not say to Jonah, "Okay, into the fish with you, and I won't let you out until you've passed everything: character, thoughts about Nineveh, attitude to the lost, trusting my wisdom—the whole bit. When you get out, you'll be a sanctified man."

When you overcome one obstacle, don't think it's the only issue in your life God wants to sort out. Don't assume, "I've arrived." God will simply say, "Well, I'm glad you're out of that.

Now you can turn over the page and have a look at the next thing I want to say to you." When you have conquered one peak, another beckons. Sanctification isn't an instant magic trick. It's an ongoing, step-by-step relationship with God.

God keeps working on people

Jonah was an obnoxious character. He was delivered from the fish and saw a great revival, but still he missed the point. God could so easily have said, "That's it! You've taken up too much of my time already." But he didn't. God loved him enough to keep working on him. God really loves the unlovely and is committed to winning and transforming them.

When I look back over my own life, I am amazed at God's patience. I would have given up on myself ages ago. Maybe you feel the same way. Sometimes we think, "God, what on earth made me do that? How could I have been so unkind? How could I have said such an awful thing? It just slipped out and it must have hurt." Sometimes you are shocked by yourself and realize how selfish you are. God has always known what is underneath, but he is not deterred.

"I love to see you succeed," says God. "I'm not glorified by unfruitful Christians. Pruning produces more fruit, and I'm looking for glory on a grand scale. But outward success isn't the whole story. I want your success to be properly motivated."

In his mercy, God refused to abandon Jonah as a hopeless case. As a master craftsman he kept chiseling away at him, using first one instrument, then another, to penetrate and shape his heart.

God appoints circumstances

While Jonah sat outside Nineveh, the sun climbed high in the sky. As the temperature rose, Jonah wondered how long he would have to wait in the sweltering heat before God judged the people. God looked down on him, took pity, and "appointed a plant" (Jonah 4:6, NASB). The vine grew over Jonah and sheltered him. Jonah was naturally very happy with this expression of

God's grace. He was, however, not so happy when God, in that same grace, appointed a worm to chew through the vine and sent a scorching east wind to increase Jonah's discomfort.

In his grace, God appoints circumstances for us. Sometimes he says, "I'm giving you a plant to protect you and show you that I love you." And we say, "Thank you, Father. Now I know you love me." But sometimes, God appoints a worm to remove the shade and a scorching east wind to blow down on us. It's the same loving God at work, but he's working in a different way. His purpose is to transform us into the image of his Son, and he will appoint whatever is appropriate at the time to bring about that goal.

Have you encountered any scorching east winds recently? Maybe you are in the business world and are getting some Japanese east wind. Their product is cheaper than yours. How are you going to survive? You could do with a plant, some protection—a tariff on imported goods, perhaps. But it doesn't come. Or maybe it's a Middle East wind, and oil prices are increasing so much that your business is in jeopardy. You long for protection, but it's not there. Life is uncomfortable.

Sometimes the east wind just seems to come from nowhere. Suddenly we find that we are facing hostility and opposition, and we cry out, "What's happening to me? Lord, give me some shelter. Stop this east wind. I can't stand it!" But God replies, "No. In my love I have appointed the east wind for you. Receive it from me." But Jonah hated the wind and railed against it.

The apostle Paul's attitude to his "east wind" was totally different. What was his east wind? It was a "thorn in my flesh, a messenger of Satan, to torment me" (2 Cor. 12:7). God removed his protecting hand and allowed Satan to prevent Paul from becoming proud of his revelations. Paul asked God three times to remove it, but God replied, "My grace is sufficient for you, for my power is made perfect in weakness." The apostle joyfully accepted this because he continued, "I will boast all the more gladly about my weaknesses, so that Christ's power may rest on me" (2 Cor. 12:9).

What was Paul's thorn in the flesh? Verse ten seems to imply weaknesses, insults, hardships, and persecutions. Time and time again Paul came up against hostility. He pleaded with God to remove it, but God said no. And when Paul realized that God's strength is perfected in weakness, he declared, "Okay, Lord, I'll accept it and I'll rejoice in it." He allowed the east wind to shape his character and bring glory to God.

Since God appoints circumstances to change your character, don't fight everything that comes your way. By all means ask God to intervene, but if he does not, learn the lesson intended. Let him use the scorching heat to form the image of his Son in you—and rejoice as you go through it.

God reasons with us

Having appointed some circumstances to shape his servant, the Lord resorted to another method, namely reasoning. Jonah was in no mood for rejoicing. He was angry at the way things were turning out, and did not think twice about showing it. We would probably have left him to stew in his rebellious juice, but God did not. He drew alongside Jonah and began to reason with him. "Do you have a right to be angry about the vine?" (Jonah 4:9) God asked him. "It grew overnight and died overnight. You didn't contribute anything, did you?"

God has the authority to command us and to expect our obedience. He knows what is best and should not need to debate with anyone. But God is so merciful. Often he discusses things with his servants. "Come, let us reason together," he invites. He grants us the dignity of reasoning with him. Jesus told his disciples, "No longer do I call you servants but friends." God loved Jonah, so he tried to stop him from wallowing in his emotions by asking him to face up to a few facts.

God reveals his own heart

"Look, Jonah," said God, "You're concerned about the welfare of a little plant, so why can't I have compassion for the thousands of people in Nineveh?"

When Jesus saw the crowds, "he had compassion on them" (Matt. 9:36). When we see the crowds, they look happy enough. They look self-assured and confident, secure with their big houses, shiny cars, and all the latest gadgets. "Surely they don't need God," we may think. "They appear to be so comfortable already." But Jesus sees right through all the frills and into their hearts. He sees the anxiety of the man who is about to lose his job and the distress of the mother who can't cope with life any more. "I see them flung down" (NIV margin), he says. "And I'm filled with compassion for them."

While he was in Athens, Paul spoke to the crowds there and told them, "From one man [God] made every nation of men, that they should inhabit the whole earth; and he determined the times set for them and the exact places where they should live. God did this so that men would seek him and perhaps reach out for him and find him, though he is not far from each one of us" (Acts 17:26,27).

Here Paul was speaking not to people who had a knowledge of God, but to the heathen. They all came from one man, Adam, and God referred to Adam as his son (Luke 3:37). He saw Adam ensnared and corrupted by the enemy, and with him all the nations as well, but they are still his offspring through Adam. In God they "live and move and have [their] being" (Acts 17:28)— even though they are hardly aware of it.

Sometimes the image of God shines through ungodly people. Jonah told the sailors, "Pick me up and throw me into the sea, and it will become calm" (Jonah 1:12). At first, compassion prevented them. They tried their hardest to save him. In much the same way, people today often display kindness to relieve others of their suffering. Indeed, even the toughest individual can reflect something of God's character, because he is God's offspring.

God looked with compassion on the heathen in Nineveh, recognizing that they were his offspring, captive in the hands of Satan. "Shouldn't I be concerned about them?" he questioned Jonah. Today, God looks with pity on the lost and says, "Shouldn't I be concerned about them? Yes, they're sinful, but they're my offspring. I love them, and I gave my Son to save them. I am not far from any one of them. They could hear the gospel message and respond and their lives could be changed. I want you to share my compassion and reach out to them—not with cold professionalism but with tender mercy."

So often we are more concerned about the "plants" than the people. We preoccupy ourselves with our own ministries rather than sharing God's yearning for the human race. Even our evangelism can be an "ego trip" or an endeavor to prove ourselves. We can be very like Jonah, with our motives so muddled. God wants to change and purify us so that our actions match our attitudes and there is no room for hypocrisy.

Every one of us will experience a "Jonah, chapter four." The curtain will rise and you will be alone with God. Actions will be weighed. Secret motives will be revealed. The things hidden in darkness will face the light.

How will you score when God unearths the attitudes you've kept so well concealed? Will your works stand the test of fire? God wants to reward you. It gives him no pleasure to find you out. That is why his word warns you that this final scene will certainly take place for you—with you as the star of the drama!

Be motivated by that. Let God search your motives now. Develop accountability to others now. Prepare to meet your God. Christ is coming for a bride who has made herself ready, adorned for her husband. Get involved in actions motivated by love and faith that he will delight to reward.

"Behold, I am coming soon! My reward is with me, and I will give to everyone according to what he has done" (Rev. 22:12).

CONCLUSION

LIMPING ARMY, INVINCIBLE COMMANDER

Each of our three heroes is seen at his most vulnerable. The Bible makes no attempt to conceal their weaknesses. Rather the opposite: their failures are recorded in graphic detail.

David, without hesitation, yields to his fleshly appetite and, taking advantage of his privileged position of power, tries to cover his tracks in the most cowardly and callous way. Elijah is transformed from powerhouse to puny mouse. One minute he is courageous, the next he is terrified; once preoccupied with God's glory, now with self-preservation; once standing firm, now running scared; once dictating history, now irrelevant; once public and visible, now hiding in the wilderness; once crystal clear about issues, now thoroughly muddled and suicidal.

And what can we say about Jonah? Is there anything to recommend him? Perhaps this, that he recorded the whole story for us to read. Only he could have told it, for only he was there. Perhaps we should not despise him for his weakness but love him for his amazing honesty, for letting his private diary be read by all. He must finally have understood what God was doing to him and how ugly his character was in order to record the whole drama in such detail. We can only assume that even Jonah "made it" in the end.

Surely here is the point of these accounts. God took hold of three vulnerable people and accomplished amazing things through them. Having done that, he wants you not to be overwhelmed and feel disqualified by their exploits and triumphs, but to be encouraged that if God can use people like this, he can certainly use you. Here is clear proof that his strength is made perfect in weakness.

Jesus declared that the meek would inherit the earth. The arrogant and powerful are not going to do it, though it seems they could. If we feel self-assured, God will deal with us. Scheming Jacob was turned into mighty Israel, the Prince with God, not by a course in developing self-confidence, but by learning to limp and lean on his staff. Meek and mighty Jesus will inherit the earth aided and abetted by what Eric Delve calls his "limping army." Guess who gets the glory? Guess who deserves the glory?

Sometimes God's servants come very close to receiving glory. "David has slain his ten thousands," they sang. The name "Elijah" means "the Lord is God." When the fire fell from heaven and consumed the sacrifice, tens of thousands shouted, "The Lord is God! The Lord is God!" Perhaps it sounded like, "Elijah, Elijah!" At Jonah's preaching the whole population of a vast city turned around in total repentance. It's all pretty heady stuff. Who can live with it?

When asked how he manages to remain so humble, a man with a high-profile ministry tells a story. He invites his listeners to imagine a donkey, the one on which Jesus rode into Jerusalem on Palm Sunday, returning to his stable later that evening and being greeted by his fellow donkeys. "You'll never guess what happened to me today," he says. "I walked into Jerusalem and enormous crowds gathered around me. They threw their clothes under my feet and cut down leaves and branches from the trees for me to walk on. They shouted out, 'Blessed is he who comes in the name of the Lord!' But you'll never believe what else they shouted. They want me to be king of Israel!" Turning to his long-eared companions, he asks, "Do you think I should accept? Think what it will mean for our species!"

Only a donkey would imagine that the one who simply carries the word of God deserves the glory.

Those who are fully acquainted with their total vulnerability have no illusions. They know that "without him, I can do nothing." Jesus limited himself to the "likeness of sinful flesh" and showed us the way by living in absolute dependence on his Father, and told us, "Blessed are the poor in spirit, for theirs is the kingdom of heaven." Mary added, "The rich he has sent empty away."

Unqualified but not disqualified

But this is not weakness to grovel in and make us abandon all hope. The very opposite takes place. Those who recognize that they are fundamentally weak and unqualified for the task cast themselves more wholeheartedly on an all-sufficient God. They get close to him. They enjoy ever-increasing intimacy and revelation of his power, his purpose, and his amazing grace. In the end your ministry is your view of the grace of God and the power of the Holy Spirit, and this view expands when you experience increasing fellowship with Jesus.

The thirsty world is parched and longing for Christians who enjoy intimate fellowship with God. The world's need will never be met by church committees or by our latest endeavors to prove that we are "modern and relevant." Christians who put all their confidence in being as much like the world as possible have missed the point. When we prove we can have as good a rock band as the world, we have proved nothing. When our young people are trying to win an audience simply by trying to sound like their modern contemporaries or look like them, they have failed to take note of biblical principles.

Of course, there is no point in simply wearing clothes that are ten years out of date to prove that you are not worldly. There must be a genuine identification with our generation and a meaningful incarnation of truth. But do catch the impact of the other great truth that David, Elijah, and Jonah teach us, namely, that their identification with their generation was less important than their fellowship with God.

When David came from secret fellowship with God, he was baffled by the Israelites' attitude to Goliath. "Who is this uncircumcised Philistine?" he asked with incredulity. What sounded like naivete to Saul's soldiers was in fact pure unadulterated faith in the living God. Nor were they mere words, as Goliath was soon to discover.

Though Elijah appeared to have come from nowhere, he actually came from the presence of God, "before whom he stood." With uncompromising confidence he took control of the situation. He made no pretense of "appreciating other points of view and modern perspectives." He came from God and was in no doubt about his instructions. He bowed to a higher authority and was unmoved by his contemporaries. When will the church start looking like men sent from God?

Jonah had no credentials at all. Backsliding was his strong suit. But he knew this, that God had sent him. He had total faith in his message and in the God who had apprehended and commissioned him.

Jesus said to his disciples, "As the Father sent me, so send I you." Weak and vulnerable disciples backed and accompanied by an invincible Savior turned the world upside down. As the end draws near and the scene is set for world upheaval, make sure you play your part. Make sure you are ready for Christ's appearing by doing the works he has given you to do, confident in your all-sufficient Savior. We are weak in our humanity, but we have a mighty God.

Also from Cityhill Publishing...

Living God's Way by Arthur Wallis
A study manual for understanding basic concepts of the Christian life.

On To Maturity by Arthur Wallis
An insightful and practical study course applying Bible truths to the challenges we face every day.

China Miracle by Arthur Wallis
A fast-moving account of the church in China, yesterday and today.

In The Day of Thy Power by Arthur Wallis
A picture of revival in Scripture and history.

Queen Take Your Throne by Eileen Wallis
Drawing from the life of Queen Esther, this set of 16 Bible studies offers sensible answers for today's women.

Pocket Principles for Leaders by Costa Deir
Designed to fit the businessman's inside coat pocket, each book in this five-volume set contains concise capsules of wisdom for today's leaders.

Lives in Focus edited by Richard Myhre
Fourteen profiles of ordinary people who find meaning through a relationship with Jesus Christ. Presents the gospel through autobiographical stories.

These books are available from your local Christian bookstore or direct from the publisher:
Cityhill Publishing
4600 Christian Fellowship Road
Columbia, MO 65203
For Visa and Mastercard orders, call 1-800-733-8093.